Colorado Rockies 2020

A Baseball Companion

Edited by R.J. Anderson, Craig Goldstein and Bret Sayre

Baseball Prospectus

Craig Brown, Steven Goldman and David Pease, Consultant Editors
Robert Au, Harry Pavlidis and Amy Pircher, Statistics Editors

Copyright © 2020 by DIY Baseball, LLC.
All rights reserved

This book or any part thereof may not be reproduced or transmitted in any form or by any means, electronic or mechanical, including photocopying, recording, or by any information storage and retrieval system, without permission in writing from the publisher.

Limit of Liability/Disclaimer of Warranty: While the publisher and the author have used their best efforts in preparing this book, they make no representations or warranties with respect to the accuracy or completeness of the contents of this book and specifically disclaim any implied warranties of merchantability or fitness for a particular purpose. No warranty may be created or extended by sales representatives or written sales materials. The advice and strategies contained herein may not be suitable for your situation. You should consult with a professional where appropriate. Neither the publisher nor the author shall be liable for any loss of profit or any other commercial damages, including but not limited to special, incidental, consequential, or other damages.

Library of Congress Cataloging-in-Publication Data:
paperback
ISBN-13: 978-1-950716-02-9

Project Credits
Cover Design: Michael Byzewski at Aesthetic Apparatus
Interior Design and Production: Jeff Pease, Dave Pease
Layout: Jeff Pease, Dave Pease

Baseball icon courtesy of Uberux, from https://www.shareicon.net/author/uberux

Ballpark diagram courtesy of Lou Spirito/THIRTY81 Project, https://thirty81project.com/

Manufactured in the United States of America
10 9 8 7 6 5 4 3 2 1

Table of Contents

Statistical Introduction v

Part 1: Team Analysis

Colorado Rockies: Where Are You Going, Where Have You Been? 3
  Ginny Searle, Wilson Karaman and Matthew Trueblood

Performance Graphs 7

2019 Team Performance 8

2020 Team Projections 9

Team Personnel 10

Coors Field Stats 11

Rockies Team Analysis 13

Part 2: Player Analysis

Rockies Player Analysis 20

Rockies Prospects 101

Part 3: Featured Articles

The Baseball Is Juiced (Again) 115
  Robert Arthur

The Moral Hazard of Playing It Safe 119
  Craig Goldstein

Index of Names 125

Statistical Introduction

Sports are, fundamentally, a blend of athletic endeavor and storytelling. Baseball, like any other sport, tells its stories in so many ways: in the arc of a game from the stands or a season from the box scores, in photos, or even in numbers. At Baseball Prospectus, we understand that statistics don't replace observation or any of baseball's stories, but complement everything else that makes the game so much fun.

What stats help us with is with patterns and precision, variance and value. This book can help you learn things you may not see from watching a game or hundred, whether it's the path of a career over time or the breadth of the entire MLB. We'd also never ask you to choose between our numbers and the experience of viewing a game from the cheap seats or the comfort of your home; our publication combines running the numbers with observations and wisdom from some of the brightest minds we can find. But if you *do* want to learn more about the numbers beyond what's on the backs of player jerseys, let us help explain.

Offense

We've revised our methodology for determining batting value. Long-time readers of the book will notice that we've retired True Average in favor of a new metric: Deserved Runs Created Plus (DRC+). Developed by Jonathan Judge and our stats team, this statistic measures everything a player does at the plate–reaching base, hitting for power, making outs, and moving runners over–and puts it on a scale where 100 equals league-average performance. A DRC+ of 150 is terrific, a DRC+ of 100 is average and a DRC+ of 75 means you better be an excellent defender.

DRC+ also does a better job than any of our previous metrics in taking contextual factors into account. The model adjusts for how the park affects performance, but also for things like the talent of the opposing pitcher, value of different types of batted-ball events, league, temperature and other factors. It's able to describe a player's expected offensive contribution than any other statistic we've found over the years, and also does a better job of predicting future performance as well.

There's a lot more to DRC+'s story, and you can read all about it in greater depth near the end of this book.

The other aspect of run-scoring is baserunning, which we quantify using Baserunning Runs. BRR not only records the value of stolen bases (or getting caught in the act), but also accounts for all the stuff that doesn't show up on the back of a baseball card: a runner's ability to go first to third on a single, or advance on a fly ball.

Defense

Where offensive value is *relatively* easy to identify and understand, defensive value is...not. Over the past dozen years, the sabermetric community has focused mostly on stats based on zone data: a real-live human person records the type of batted ball and estimated landing location, and models are created that give expected outs. From there, you can compare fielders' actual outs to those expected ones. Simple, right?

Unfortunately, zone data has two major issues. First, zone data is recorded by commercial data providers who keep the raw data private unless you pay for it. (All the statistics we build in this book and on our website use public data as inputs.) That hurts our ability to test assumptions or duplicate results. Second, over the years it has become apparent that there's quite a bit of "noise" in zone-based fielding analysis. Sometimes the conclusions drawn from zone data don't hold up to scrutiny, and sometimes the different data provided by different providers don't look anything alike, giving wildly different results. Sometimes the hard-working professional stringers or scorers might unknowingly inflict unconscious bias into the mix: for example good fielders will often be credited with more expected outs despite the data, and ballparks with high press boxes tend to score more line drives than ones with a lower press box.

Enter our Fielding Runs Above Average (FRAA). For most positions, FRAA is built from play-by-play data, which allows us to avoid the subjectivity found in many other fielding metrics. The idea is this: count how many fielding plays are made by a given player and compare that to expected plays for an average fielder at their position (based on pitcher ground ball tendencies and batter handedness). Then we adjust for park and base-out situations.

When it comes to catchers, our methodology is a little different thanks to the laundry list of responsibilities they're tasked with beyond just, well, catching and throwing the ball. By now you've probably heard about "framing" or the art of making umpires more likely to call balls outside the strike zone for strikes. To put this into one tidy number, we incorporate pitch tracking data (for the years it exists) and adjust for important factors like pitcher, umpire, batter and home-field advantage using a mixed-model approach. This grants us a number for how many strikes the catcher is personally adding to (or subtracting from) his pitchers' performance...which we then convert to runs added or lost using linear weights.

Framing is one of the biggest parts of determining catcher value, but we also take into account blocking balls from going past, whether a scorer deems it a passed ball or a wild pitch. We use a similar approach—one that really benefits from the pitch tracking data that tells us what ends up in the dirt and what doesn't. We also include a catcher's ability to prevent stolen bases and how well they field balls in play, and *finally* we come up with our FRAA for catchers.

Pitching

Both pitching and fielding make up the half of baseball that isn't run scoring: run prevention. Separating pitching from fielding is a tough task, and most recent pitching analysis has branched off from Voros McCracken's famous (and controversial) statement, "There is little if any difference among major-league pitchers in their ability to prevent hits on balls hit in the field of play." The research of the analytic community has validated this to some extent, and there are a host of "defense-independent" pitching measures that have been developed to try and extract the effect of the defense behind a hurler from the pitcher's work.

Our solution to this quandary is Deserved Run Average (DRA), our core pitching metric. DRA looks like earned run average (ERA), the tried-and-true pitching stat you've seen on every baseball broadcast or box score from the past century, but it's very different. To start, DRA takes an event-by-event look at what the pitchers does, and adjusts the value of that event based on different environmental factors like park, batter, catcher, umpire, base-out situation, run differential, inning, defense, home field advantage, pitcher role and temperature. That mixed model gives us a pitcher's expected contribution, similar to what we do for our DRC+ model for hitters and FRAA model for catchers. (Oh, and we also consider the pitcher's effect on basestealing and on balls getting past the catcher.)

It's important to note that DRA is set to the scale of runs allowed per nine innings (RA9) instead of ERA, which makes DRA's scale slightly higher than ERA's. The reason for this is because ERA tends to overrate three types of pitchers:

1. Pitchers who play in parks where scorers hand out more errors. Official scorers differ significantly in the frequency at which they assign errors to fielders.
2. Ground-ball pitchers, because a substantial proportion of errors occur on groundballs.
3. Pitchers who aren't very good. Better pitchers often allow fewer unearned runs than bad pitchers, because good pitchers tend to find ways to get out of jams.

Since the last time you picked up an edition of this book, we've also made a few minor changes to DRA to make it better. Recent research into "tunneling"—the act of throwing consecutive pitches that appear similar from a batter's point of view until after the swing decision point–data has given us a new contextual factor to account for in DRA: plate distance. This refers to the distance between successive pitches as they approach the plate, and while it has a smaller effect than factors like velocity or whiff rate, it still can help explain pitcher strikeout rate in our model.

New Pitching Metrics for 2020

We're including a few "new" pitching metrics in the book for the 2020 edition, though unlike last year, these numbers may be a little bit more familiar to those of you who have spent some time investigating baseball statistics.

Fastball Percentage

Our fastball percentage (FB%) statistic measures how frequently a pitcher throws a pitch classified as a "fastball," measured as a percentage of overall pitches thrown. We qualify three types of fastballs:

1. The traditional four-seam fastball;
2. The two-seam fastball or sinker;
3. "Hard cutters," which are pitches that have the movement profile of a cut fastball and are used as the pitcher's primary offering or in place of a more traditional fastball.

For example, a pitcher with a FB% of 67 throws any combination of these three pitches about two-thirds of the time.

Whiff Rate

Everybody loves a swing and a miss, and whiff rate (WHF) measures how frequently pitchers induce a swinging strike. To calculate WHF, we add up all the pitches thrown that ended with a swinging strike, then divide that number by a pitcher's total pitches thrown. Most often, high whiff rates correlate with high strikeout rates (and overall effective pitcher performance).

Called Strike Probability

Called Strike Probability (CSP) is a number that represents the likelihood that all of a pitcher's pitches will be called a strike while controlling for location, pitcher and batter handedness, umpire and count. Here's how it works: on each pitch, our model determines how many times (out of 100) that a similar pitch was called for a strike given those factors mentioned above, and when normalized for each batter's strike zone. Then we average the CSP for all pitches thrown by a pitcher in a season, and that gives us the yearly CSP percentage you see in the stats boxes.

As you might imagine, pitchers with a higher CSP are more likely to work in the zone, where pitchers with a lower CSP are likely locating their pitches outside the normal strike zone, for better or for worse.

Projections

Many of you aren't turning to this book just for a look at what a player has done, but for a look at what a player is going to do: the PECOTA projections. PECOTA, initially developed by Nate Silver (who has moved on to greater fame as a political analyst), consists of three parts:

1. Major-league equivalencies, which use minor-league statistics to project how a player will perform in the major leagues;
2. Baseline forecasts, which use weighted averages and regression to the mean to estimate a player's current true talent level; and
3. Aging curves, which uses the career paths of comparable players to estimate how a player's statistics are likely to change over time.

With all those important things covered, let's take a look at what's in the book this year.

Team Prospectus

Most of this book is composed of team chapters, with one for each of the 30 major-league franchises. On the first page of each chapter, you'll see a box that contains some of the key statistics for each team as well as a very inviting stadium diagram. (You can see an example of this for the Milwaukee Brewers on this very page!)

We start with the team name, their unadjusted 2019 win-loss record, and their divisional ranking. Beneath that are a host of other team statistics. **Pythag** presents an adjusted 2019 winning percentage, calculated by taking runs scored per game (**RS/G**) and runs allowed per game (**RA/G**) for the team, and running them through a version of Bill James' Pythagorean formula that was refined and improved by David Smyth and Brandon Heipp. (The formula is called "Pythagenpat," which is equally fun to type and to say.)

Next up is **DRC+**, described earlier, to indicate the overall hitting ability of the team either above or below league-average. Run prevention on the pitching side is covered by **DRA** (also mentioned earlier) and another metric: Fielding Independent Pitching (**FIP**), which calculates another ERA-like statistic based on strikeouts, walks, and home runs recorded. Defensive Efficiency Rating (**DER**) tells us the percentage of balls in play turned into outs for the team, and is a quick fielding shorthand that rounds out run prevention.

After that, we have several measures related to roster composition, as opposed to on-field performance. **B-Age** and **P-Age** tell us the average age of a team's batters and pitchers, respectively. **Salary** is the combined team payroll for all on-field players, and Doug Pappas' Marginal Dollars per Marginal Win (**M$/MW**) tells us how much money a team spent to earn production above replacement level.

Ending this batch of statistics is the number of disabled list days a team had over the season (**IL Days**) and the amount of salary paid to players on the disabled list (**$ on IL**); this final number is expressed as a percentage of total payroll.

Next to each of these stats, we've listed each team's MLB rank in that category from first to 30th. In this, first always indicates a positive outcome and 30th a negative outcome, except in the case of salary—first is highest.

After the franchise statistics, we share a few items about the team's home ballpark. There's the aforementioned diagram of the park's dimensions (including distances to the outfield wall), a graphic showing the height of the wall from the left-field pole to the right-field pole, and a table showing three-year park factors for the stadium. The park factors are displayed as indexes where 100 is average, 110 means that the park inflates the statistic in question by 10 percent, and 90 means that the park deflates the statistic in question by 10 percent.

On the second page of each team chapter, you'll find three graphs. The first is the **2019 Hit List Ranking**. This shows our Hit List Rank for the team on each day of the 2019 season and is intended to give you a picture of the ups and downs of the team's season. Hit List Rank measures overall team performance and drives the Hit List Power Rankings at the baseballprospectus.com website.

The second graph is **Committed Payroll** and helps you see how the team's payroll has compared to the MLB and divisional average payrolls over time. Payroll figures are current as of January 1, 2020; with so many free agents still unsigned as of this writing, the final 2020 figure will likely be significantly different for many teams. (In the meantime, you can always find the most current data at Baseball Prospectus' Cot's Baseball Contracts page.)

The third graph is **Farm System Ranking** and displays how the Baseball Prospectus prospect team has ranked the organization's farm system since 2007.

After the graphs, we have a **Personnel** section that lists many of the important decision-makers and upper-level field and operations staff members for the franchise, as well as any former Baseball Prospectus staff members who are currently part of the organization. (In very rare circumstances, someone might be on both lists!)

Juan Soto LF

Born: 10/25/98 Age: 21 Bats: L Throws: L
Height: 6'1" Weight: 185 Origin: International Free Agent, 2015

YEAR	TEAM	LVL	AGE	PA	R	2B	3B	HR	RBI	BB	K	SB	CS	AVG/OBP/SLG
2017	NAT	RK	18	27	3	1	1	0	4	2	1	0	0	.320/.370/.440
2017	HAG	A	18	96	15	5	0	3	14	10	8	1	2	.360/.427/.523
2018	HAG	A	19	74	12	5	3	5	24	14	13	2	0	.373/.486/.814
2018	POT	A+	19	73	17	3	1	7	18	11	8	0	1	.371/.466/.790
2018	HAR	AA	19	35	4	2	0	2	10	4	7	1	0	.323/.400/.581
2018	WAS	MLB	19	494	77	25	1	22	70	79	99	5	2	.292/.406/.517
2019	WAS	MLB	20	659	110	32	5	34	110	108	132	12	1	.282/.401/.548
2020	WAS	MLB	21	630	92	30	3	35	102	85	123	5	2	.284/.382/.543

Comparables: Ronald Acuña Jr., Mike Trout, Tony Conigliaro

YEAR	TEAM	LVL	AGE	PA	DRC+	VORP	BABIP	BRR	FRAA	WARP
2017	NAT	RK	18	27	135	1.5	.333	0.0	RF(9): -1.1	0.0
2017	HAG	A	18	96	181	8.0	.373	1.0	RF(19): -1.9, LF(2): -0.3	0.9
2018	HAG	A	19	74	222	14.5	.405	0.3	RF(14): 1.1, CF(2): 0.2	1.2
2018	POT	A+	19	73	260	15.4	.340	1.4	RF(14): 1.0, LF(1): 0.0	1.6
2018	HAR	AA	19	35	113	3.6	.364	0.0	LF(4): 0.6, RF(4): -0.5	0.1
2018	WAS	MLB	19	494	125	40.5	.338	-0.5	LF(114): 2.7	3.0
2019	WAS	MLB	20	659	136	49.0	.312	1.4	LF(150): -0.8	4.9
2020	WAS	MLB	21	630	133	43.6	.310	-0.1	LF 3	4.8

Position Players

After all that information and a thoughtful bylined essay covering each team, we present our player comments. These are also bylined, but due to frequent franchise shifts during the offseason, our bylines are more a rough guide than a perfect accounting of who wrote what.

Each player is listed with the major-league team that employed him as of early January 2020. If a player changed teams after that point via free agency, trade, or any other method, you'll be able to find them in the chapter for their previous squad.

As an example, take a look at the player comment for Nationals outfielder Juan Soto: the stat block that accompanies his written comment is at the top of this page. First we cover biographical information (age is as of June 30, 2020) before moving onto the stats themselves. Our statistic columns include standard identifying information like **YEAR**, **TEAM**, **LVL** (level of affiliated play) and **AGE** before getting into the numbers. Next, we provide raw, untranslated numbers like you might find on the back of your dad's baseball cards: **PA** (plate appearances), **R** (runs), **2B** (doubles), **3B** (triples), **HR** (home runs), **RBI** (runs batted in), **BB** (walks), **K** (strikeouts), **SB** (stolen bases) and **CS** (caught stealing).

Next, we have unadjusted "slash" statistics: **AVG** (batting average), **OBP** (on-base percentage) and **SLG** (slugging percentage). Following the slash line is **DRC+** (Deserved Runs Created Plus), which we described earlier as total offensive expected contribution compared to the league average.

One of our oldest active metrics, **VORP** (Value Over Replacement Player), considers offensive production, position and plate appearances. In essence, it is the number of runs contributed beyond what a replacement-level player at the same position would contribute if given the same percentage of team plate appearances. VORP does not consider the quality of a player's defense.

BABIP (batting average on balls in play) tells us how often a ball in play fell for a hit, and can help us identify whether a batter may have been lucky or not…but note that high BABIPs also tend to follow the great hitters of our time, as well as speedy singles hitters who put the ball on the ground.

The next item is **BRR** (Baserunning Runs), which covers all of a player's baserunning accomplishments including (but not limited to) swiped bags and failed attempts. Next is **FRAA** (Fielding Runs Above Average), which also includes the number of games previously played at each position noted in parentheses. Multi-position players have only their two most frequent positions listed here, but their total FRAA number reflects all positions played.

Our last column here is **WARP** (Wins Above Replacement Player). WARP estimates the total value of a player, which means for hitters it takes into account hitting runs above average (calculated using the DRC+ model), BRR and FRAA. Then, it makes an adjustment for positions played and gives the player a credit for plate appearances based upon the difference between "replacement level"—which is derived from the quality of players added to a team's roster after the start of the season–and the league average.

The final line just below the stats box is **PECOTA** data, which is discussed further in a following section.

Catchers

Catchers are a special breed, and thus they have earned their own separate box which displays some of the defensive metrics that we've built just for them. As an example, let's check out J.T. Realmuto.

The **YEAR** and **TEAM** columns match what you'd find in the other stat box. **P. COUNT** indicates the number of pitches thrown while the catcher was behind the plate, including swinging strikes, fouls and balls in play. **FRM RUNS** is the total run value the catcher provided (or cost) his team by influencing the umpire to call strikes where other catchers did not. **BLK RUNS** expresses the total run value above or below average for the catcher's ability to prevent wild pitches and passed balls. **THRW RUNS** is calculated using a similar model as the previous two statistics, and it measures a catcher's ability to throw out basestealers but also to dissuade them from testing his arm in the first place. It takes into account factors like the pitcher (including his delivery and pickoff move) and baserunner (who could be as fast as Billy Hamilton or as slow as Yonder Alonso). **TOT RUNS** is the sum of all of the previous three statistics.

Justin Verlander RHP

Born: 02/20/83 Age: 37 Bats: R Throws: R
Height: 6'5" Weight: 225 Origin: Round 1, 2004 Draft (#2 overall)

YEAR	TEAM	LVL	AGE	W	L	SV	G	GS	IP	H	HR	BB/9	K/9	K	GB%	BABIP
2017	DET	MLB	34	10	8	0	28	28	172	153	23	3.5	9.2	176	34%	.283
2017	HOU	MLB	34	5	0	0	5	5	34	17	4	1.3	11.4	43	32%	.194
2018	HOU	MLB	35	16	9	0	34	34	214	156	28	1.6	12.2	290	31%	.272
2019	HOU	MLB	36	21	6	0	34	34	223	137	36	1.7	12.1	300	36%	.219
2020	HOU	MLB	37	15	6	0	29	29	184	138	28	2.3	12.1	248	35%	.274

Comparables: Zack Greinke, A.J. Burnett, Aníbal Sánchez

YEAR	TEAM	LVL	AGE	WHIP	ERA	DRA	WARP	MPH	FB%	WHF	CSP
2017	DET	MLB	34	1.28	3.82	4.03	3.0	97.7	58	11	47.8
2017	HOU	MLB	34	0.65	1.06	3.08	0.9	97.5	59.6	15.1	49.9
2018	HOU	MLB	35	0.90	2.52	2.33	7.3	97.5	61.2	16.2	51.6
2019	HOU	MLB	36	0.80	2.58	2.51	7.9	96.8	49.9	17.5	48.3
2020	HOU	MLB	37	1.01	2.75	2.95	5.3	95.8	54.6	15.1	48.2

Pitchers

Let's give our pitchers a turn, using 2019 AL Cy Young winner Justin Verlander as our example. Take a look at his stat block: the first line and the **YEAR**, **TEAM**, **LVL** and **AGE** columns are the same as in the position player example earlier.

Here too, we have a series of columns that display raw, unadjusted statistics compiled by the pitcher over the course of a season: **W** (wins), **L** (losses), **SV** (saves), **G** (games pitched), **GS** (games started), **IP** (innings pitched), **H** (hits allowed) and **HR** (home runs allowed). Next we have two statistics that are rates: **BB/9** (walks per nine innings) and **K/9** (strikeouts per nine innings), before returning to the unadjusted K (strikeouts).

Next up is **GB%** (ground ball percentage), which is the percentage of all batted balls that were hit on the ground, including both outs and hits. Remember, this is based on observational data and subject to human error, so please approach this with a healthy dose of skepticism.

BABIP (batting average on balls in play) is calculated using the same methodology as it is for position players, but it often tells us more about a pitcher than it does a hitter. With pitchers, a high BABIP is often due to poor defense or bad luck, and can often be an indicator of potential rebound, and a low BABIP may be cause to expect performance regression. (A typical league-average BABIP is close to .290-.300.)

Colorado Rockies 2020

The metrics **WHIP** (walks plus hits per inning pitched) and **ERA** (earned run average) are old standbys: WHIP measures walks and hits allowed on a per-inning basis, while ERA measures earned runs on a nine-inning basis. Neither of these stats are translated or adjusted.

DRA (Deserved Run Average) was described at length earlier, and measures how many runs the pitcher "deserved" to allow per nine innings. Please note that since we lack all the data points that would make for a "real" DRA for minor-league events, the DRA displayed for minor league partial-seasons is based off of different data. (That data is a modified version of our cFIP metric, which you can find more information about on our website.)

Just like with hitters, **WARP** (Wins Above Replacement Player) is a total value metric that puts pitchers of all stripes on the same scale as position players. We use DRA as the primary input for our calculation of WARP. You might notice that relief pitchers (due to their limited innings) may have a lower WARP than you were expecting or than you might see in other WARP-like metrics. WARP does not take leverage into account, just the actions a pitcher performs and the expected value of those actions...which ends up judging high-leverage relief pitchers differently than you might imagine given their prestige and market value.

MPH gives you the pitcher's 95th percentile velocity for the noted season, in order to give you an idea of what the *peak* fastball velocity a pitcher possesses. Since this comes from our pitch-tracking data, it is not publicly available for minor-league pitchers.

Finally, we display the three new pitching metrics we described earlier. **FB%** (fastball percentage) gives you the percentage of fastballs thrown out of all pitches. **WHF** (whiff rate) tells you the percentage of swinging strikes induced out of all pitches. **CSP** (called strike probability) expresses the likelihood of all pitches thrown to result in a called strike, after controlling for factors like handedness, umpire, pitch type, count and location.

PECOTA

All players have PECOTA projections for 2020, as well as a set of other numbers that describe the performance of comparable players according to PECOTA. All projections for 2020 are for the player at the date we went to press in early January and are projected into the league and park context as indicated by the team abbreviation. (Note that players at very low levels of the minors are too unpredictable to assess using these numbers.) All PECOTA projected statistics represent a player's projected major-league performance.

Below the projections are the player's three highest-scoring comparable players as determined by PECOTA. All comparables represent a snapshot of how the listed player was performing at the same age as the current player, so if a

23-year-old pitcher is compared to Bartolo Colón, he's actually being compared to a 23-year-old Colón, not the version that pitched for the Rangers in 2018, nor to Colón's career as a whole.

A few points about pitcher projections. First, we aren't yet projecting peak velocity, so that column will be blank in the PECOTA lines. Second, projecting DRA is trickier than evaluating past performance, because it is unclear how deserving each pitcher will be of his anticipated outcomes. However, we know that another DRA-related statistic–contextual FIP or cFIP-estimates future run scoring very well. So for PECOTA, the projected DRA figures you see are based on the past cFIPs generated by the pitcher and comparable players over time, along with the other factors described above.

Lineouts

In each chapter's Lineouts section, you'll find abbreviated text comments, as well as all the same information you'd find in our full player comments. The only difference is that we limit the stats boxes in this section to only including the 2019 information for each player.

Managers

After all those wonderful team chapters, we've got statistics for each big-league manager, all of whom are organized by alphabetical order. Here you'll find a block including an extraordinary amount of information collected from each manager's entire career. For more information on the acronyms and what they mean, please visit the Glossary at www.baseballprospectus.com.

There is one important metric that we'd like to call attention to, and you'll find it next to each manager's name: **wRM+** (weighted reliever management plus). Developed by Rob Arthur and Rian Watt, wRM+ investigates how good a manager is at using their best relievers during the moments of highest leverage, using both our proprietary DRA metric as well as Leverage Index. wRM+ is scaled to a league average of 100, and a wRM+ of 105 indicates that relievers were used approximately five percent "better" than average. On the other hand, a wRM+ of 95 would tell us the team used its relievers five percent "worse" than the average team.

While wRM+ does not have an extremely strong correlation with a manager, it is statistically significant; this means that a manager is not *entirely* responsible for a team's wRM+, but does have some effect on that number.

PECOTA Leaderboards

If you're familiar with PECOTA, then you'll have noticed that the projection system often appears bullish on players coming off a bad year and bearish on players coming off a good year. (This is because the system weights several previous seasons, not just the most recent one.) In addition, we publish the 50th

Colorado Rockies 2020

percentile projections for each player–which is smack in the middle of the range of projected production—which tends to mean PECOTA stat lines don't often have extreme results like 40 home runs or 250 strikeouts in a given season. In essence, PECOTA doesn't project very many extreme seasons.

At the end of the book, we've ranked the top players at each position based on their PECOTA projections. This might help you visualize just how a given player's projection compares to that of their peers, so that even if a dramatic stat line isn't projected, you can still imagine how they stack up against the rest of the league.

Part 1: Team Analysis

Colorado Rockies: Where Are You Going, Where Have You Been?

Ginny Searle, Wilson Karaman and Matthew Trueblood

2019: What Went Right
At the top end, at least, the Rockies did not disappoint. The homegrown trio of Nolan Arenado, Charlie Blackmon, and Trevor Story were projected for a combined 13.2 WARP and finished with 15 WARP. Despite Blackmon's collapse in defensive value putting him more in the plus-regular than All-Star category, Story made up the two wins the team's erstwhile center fielder lost off his projection. Despite a backslide to a DRC+ of 118, the shortstop has boosted his value as a strong baserunner and defender. Ryan McMahon and David Dahl (provided he can finally stay healthy) proved themselves average regulars, though the team is still a way from weaning itself of the stars-and-scrubs reliance that has characterized the last several seasons.

On the pitching side, Jairo Díaz was finally healthy and pitched well (1.2 WARP on a 3.49 DRA). Scott Oberg continued to prove himself a valuable bullpen piece (with his 3.31 DRA near-identical to Díaz's) before losing his season to a blood clot in his pitching arm. Jon Gray had his best season, with 2.9 WARP across 150 innings before going down with a season-ending injury, a fate also met by German Márquez and Tyler Anderson and Brendan Rodgers...and...

2019: What Went Wrong
The Rockies were projected to win 84 games and were hoping to build off a 2018 in which they won 91 games and forced a playoff for the NL West crown. Instead, they needed to sweep their season-ending series with the Brewers to finish at 71-91. What happened since the start of July, when they looked like staunch Wild Card competitors, besides a 27-51 record?

Let's start with Ian Desmond. The handsomest Rockie had been splashing about in the replacement-level pool since signing with Colorado, but Daniel Murphy displaced him from first base, and the slotting of Blackmon from center to right dictated Desmond's new position. The result of Desmond appearing in center for nearly half of the Rockies' innings? A -15.7 FRAA, the third-worst in the majors. That really isn't what you want in the massive expanses of the Coors outfield. Desmond has two more seasons and $25 million remaining of his five-year, $70 million pact, and literally nothing about the Rockies suggests they'll do what's wise and DFA him.

The acquisition of Murphy, Desmond's replacement at first base, was lauded by many who believed a 34-year-old second baseman forced by lack of mobility to move to first was a solid investment. Murphy's basically league-average bat didn't solve a first-base problem that, the Justin Morneau interregnum of 2014 aside, has lingered on since Todd Helton's decline. Chris Iannetta hit—or, more accurately, walked—at a rate so far below his standard he lost his job and then his roster spot. Raimel Tapia has the bat of a fourth outfielder; even with Mike Tauchman three years Tapia's senior, the team would surely exchange the two given the chance. Yonathan Daza and Noel Cuevas have not impressed in limited auditions.

And then there's the rotation. The entire—yes, all five of them—rotation that began the season spent significant time on the injured list. Gray, Márquez, Tyler Anderson, Chad Bettis, and Kyle Freeland made 83 starts. The remainder were shared by Antonio Senzatela (25 GS), Peter Lambert (19), Jeff Hoffman (15) Chi Chi González (12), Tim Melville (7), and Rico Garcia (1). Of the latter group, only Melville had an ERA under 5.00, and none had a WARP above the replacement level—cumulatively, the group finished at -5.0 WARP.

This is not to imply that injuries alone brought down the Rockies' staff; in fact, here's a black mark against each of the five starters with which the team began the season. Márquez was worth 4.7 WARP, yes, but accepting that means discounting a 4.76 ERA. Gray has now had two season-ending foot fractures in his career. Even if Anderson can get healthy, the 2011 first-rounder is a fringe fifth starter. Bettis lasted just three starts in a parchment rotation before being sent to the 'pen.

And then there's Freeland. DRA never supported Freeland's sub-3.00 ERA breakout in 2018, assigning him a mark more than an entire run above his 2.85 ERA (a DRA- roughly 15 percent better than the league average) and 3.3 WARP, a far cry from his contribution per other metrics. In 2019, Freeland saw his DRA spike two points and his ERA balloon to 6.98. He gave up eight more home runs than the year before (17) in half the innings, was demoted to the minors, and has likely significantly impacted the Rockies' future expectations of him. It would be easy to say that the clipper ball flying out of parks did in Freeland particularly, but it's just not possible for a starter to survive in today's game while allowing 10.9 hits per nine and striking out just 7.1 in the same span. Presumably, a rotation spot will be Freeland's to lose next season, but it's doubtful it will be long before it slips through his fingers.

Ultimately, what went wrong for the 2019 Rockies was that they were simply not a good baseball team despite the predictions to the contrary. Their collective 90 DRC+ was 21st in the league and their 5.38 DRA was 22nd. Those are never what you want, but given the team's sedentary winter, things may get worse before they get better. —*Ginny Searle*

Prospect Outlook

The process of evaluating Colorado's farm system can be a highly challenging exercise. There's rarely been a shortage of pipeline talent in the organization in recent years, and the system has produced plenty of star-caliber homegrown seasons of late. Trevor Story's an animal! David Dahl's been great when he's been on the field! They had that one group of pitching prospects who all broke out and were awesome at the same time for a while there!

It's a consistent soft spot below the fold, however. The organization's uber-conservative habit of a long-game partial commitment to young players—playing Raimel Tapia, Brendan Rodgers, Garrett Hampson, Ryan McMahon for a minute at a time—in favor of Pat Valaika types and Mark Reynolds retreads has been a consistent hallmark of Rockies baseball, as has an inability to build contributing depth out of an annual stockpile of bat-first corner guys. Now the next wave is sitting there, looking up at the same congested canvas their predecessors have stared upon for many moons now. **Colton Welker**, **Tyler Nevin**, **Roberto Ramos**, **Josh Fuentes** have all shown the ability to hit high-minors pitching now, but behind an entrenched Arenado. (Unless he's traded; at press time he's still with the team, but with the Rockies, who knows?)

Brendan Rodgers will contribute in some manner of regular fashion next year, and whether he can claim the keystone will be the most consequential prospect question for the club. The team also seems to have plans for outfielder **Sam Hilliard**, who got a late-season audition in '19, though he may have a fourth-outfielder ceiling. Beyond those obvious statements, the organization's ongoing challenge will again involve sifting through its bats, trying to find the good ones when they're ready to be good, and having the willpower to give them a real chance. —*Wilson Karaman*

2020 Outlook

Colorado's 2019 couldn't have gone much worse than it did on the field, but the hope was that Arenado's contract extension would give the team and its fans security and a reason to smile. That lasted about a week. It was a winter of trade rumors involving Arenado, feuds between Arenado and GM Jeff Bridich, and almost nothing else. Every other team signed a player to a guaranteed deal before the Rockies did. The idea is that, with a number of young options and a year or two left on virtually all of their bad contracts, the team might improve (and will, at least, retain flexibility) without bringing in major talent from outside the organization.

Since the team's short-, medium-, and long-term hopes all rested so heavily on Arenado, though, and since the team gave Arenado an opt-out clause after 2021, it would have been wise for them to consult with him about that strategy. Instead, the only superstar the team has had since Troy Tulowitzki was traded felt lied to and let down. Bridich didn't need to map out his entire operation for Arenado, but he needed to communicate, and he failed to. His poor bedside manner might derail the franchise for years. —*Matthew Trueblood*

Performance Graphs

2019 Hit List Ranking

Committed Payroll (in millions)

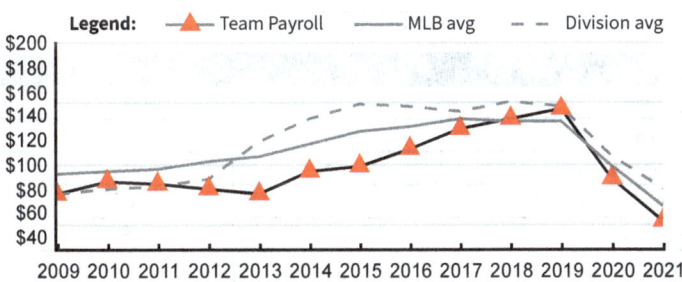

Farm System Ranking

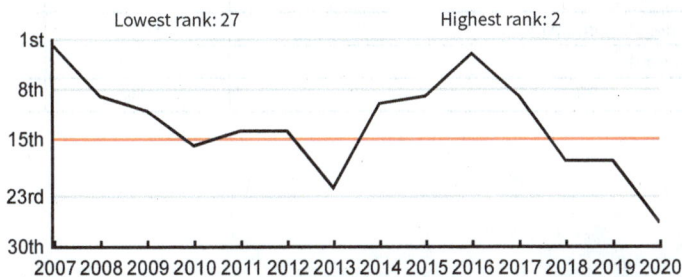

2019 Team Performance

ACTUAL STANDINGS

Team	W	L	Pct
LAN	106	56	0.654
ARI	85	77	0.525
SFN	77	85	0.475
COL	**71**	**91**	**0.438**
SDN	70	92	0.432

THIRD-ORDER STANDINGS

Team	W	L	Pct
LAN	114	48	0.702
ARI	84	78	0.516
SDN	74	88	0.454
SFN	70	92	0.431
COL	**69**	**93**	**0.429**

TOP HITTERS

Player	WARP
Nolan Arenado	7.1
Trevor Story	4.9
Charlie Blackmon	3.0

TOP PITCHERS

Player	WARP
German Márquez	4.7
Jon Gray	2.9
Scott Oberg	1.2

VITAL STATISTICS

Statistic Name	Value	Rank
Pythagenpat	.432	22nd
Runs Scored per Game	5.15	9th
Runs Allowed per Game	5.91	29th
Deserved Runs Created Plus	93	21st
Deserved Run Average	5.36	22nd
Fielding Independent Pitching	5.18	29th
Defensive Efficiency Rating	.692	24th
Batter Age	28.1	20th
Pitcher Age	26.8	3rd
Salary	$145.2M	12th
Marginal $ per Marginal Win	$5.9M	8th
Injured List Days	1018	12th
$ on IL	8%	2nd

2020 Team Projections

PROJECTED STANDINGS

Team	W	L	Pct	+/-
LAN	102.5	59.5	0.633	-4
SDN	79.3	82.7	0.490	9
ARI	78.9	83.1	0.487	-6
COL	**76.6**	**85.4**	**0.473**	**6**
SFN	68.4	93.6	0.422	-9

TOP PROJECTED HITTERS

Player	WARP
Nolan Arenado	5.4
Trevor Story	3.9
Charlie Blackmon	3.0

TOP PROJECTED PITCHERS

Player	WARP
German Márquez	2.4
Jon Gray	2.3
Carlos Estévez	0.8

FARM SYSTEM REPORT

Top Prospect	Number of Top 101 Prospects
Brendan Rodgers, #56	1

KEY DEDUCTIONS

Player	WARP
Tyler Anderson	1.1
Sam Howard	0.1
Yonder Alonso	0.0
Pat Valaika	0.0

KEY ADDITIONS

Player	WARP
Tyler Nevin	0.5
Ben Bowden	0.0
José Mujica	0.0
Ashton Goudeau	0.0
Tyler Kinley	0.0
Roberto Ramos	-0.1
Kelby Tomlinson	-0.3
Antonio Santos	-0.6

Team Personnel

General Manager
Jeff Bridich

Assistant General Manager - Baseball Operations
Zach Rosenthal

Assistant General Manager - Player Development
Zach Wilson

Assistant General Manager - Player Personnel
Jon Weil

Manager
Bud Black

Coors Field Stats

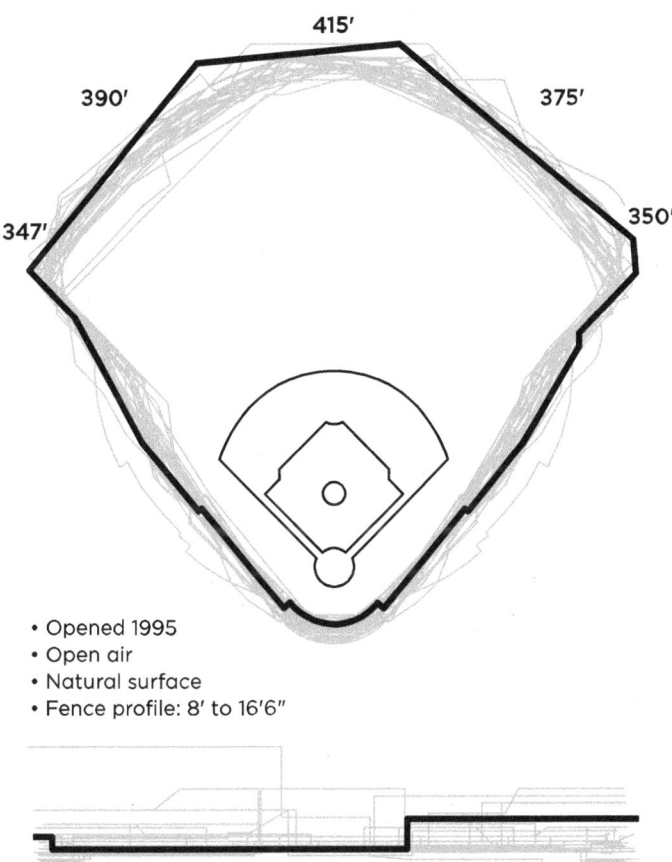

- Opened 1995
- Open air
- Natural surface
- Fence profile: 8′ to 16′6″

Three-Year Park Factors

Runs	Runs/RH	Runs/LH	HR/RH	HR/LH
112	112	112	109	111

Rockies Team Analysis

When you check into a two-star hotel room, the odds are still decent that there will be an alarm clock with an iPod dock next to the bed. There are probably features included with this clock, like the ability to wake up to whatever hot new Fall Out Boy song is on your iPod. At one point, this bold, new technology was the future. It prompted hotel managers around the country to think, yes, this is an investment that will last. This is what people will need. We should spend money on this…because it will help us *make* money.

Cut to a few years later, and that clock-radio might as well be a cassette player. No one is jamming iPods into those things in 2020. Entire generations of dust mites have come and gone, from mite cavemen to mite Mesopotamians to mite Americans, without anyone using them. Technology has advanced too far, too fast.

This is what's happened in baseball. A front office from 2010 is one of those iPod clock radios. A front office from 2020 is a phone that can stream the entire Fall Out Boy catalog to a wireless speaker at the same time you're playing *Civilization VI*. It's the future, and it makes the recent past look like the distant past.

And in 2030, when *Civilization X* is beamed directly to our brains, today's technology will seem even quainter. The front offices of 2030 will laugh at the spin-rate fetish. They'll have proprietary statistics that will prove that Yadier Molina was always more valuable than Mike Trout, and we'll just have to fall in line, shuffling and looking down at our feet, saying, "I guess this is just how baseball is now."

Baseball is hard, in other words. This ain't a game, it's a gosh dang arms race. In ten years, teams will sink if they use nothing but 2020 information. You have to keep up with the Astroses.

With that established, let's take a look at the Rockies. Not the 2020 Rockies. Not the 2019 Rockies. The Rockies as a franchise. The whole thing. If we're going to draw out the analogy even further, we have to assume that the Rockies are forever trying to figure out what the newest iPhone will be, just like the rest of baseball.

But being the only team that plays at altitude means that they're doing it all without high-speed internet. While the other 29 teams are downloading schematics and hour-long HD presentations, the Rockies are forced to listen to the connection scrrrrkkkkkhhzzzz of the 56k modem and take their chances. It's not that they're behind in the brain race. It's that they're starting with more of a disadvantage than any other team in baseball, and it's not even close.

If you think this is an unfair description, it is not. It's the Rockies' difficulty setting on this particular video game that is unfair. Baseball is hard enough, but the Rockies are forced to figure out a new branch of physics on the fly. They have to conquer something that's just as hard to conquer as baseball *at the same time they're supposed to be conquering baseball.*

That something is how to adjust for playing baseball 5,200 feet above the ocean, and it's a problem that's tormented the franchise since they've existed. They're no closer to solving it. The Rockies—the entire franchise—is the Riemann hypothesis of baseball.

The early history of the Rockies was that of an entire league realizing that hitting was very, very different at altitude. Vinny Castilla and Dante Bichette became stars and MVP candidates. Double-digit slugfests from both teams were happening once a homestand, at least. But the Rockies continually allowed more runs than they scored.

"A-ha!", someone in the Rockies' front office thought. "We need to *buy* our pitchers!"

So they tried. Mike Hampton and Denny Neagle might not have been the best test cases for this experiment—the eight years, $121 million given to Hampton would still be a huge contract for a pitcher almost 20 years later—but it's refreshing in retrospect to see an ownership group apply their profits in an effort to build a better team. Those were the days.

Didn't work.

Then there was the fascination with sinkerballers, which also made sense. Keep the ball on the ground, keep the ball in the park.

Didn't work.

Then there was a strange period where the Rockies seemed to be acquiring pitchers who didn't strike batters out on purpose. Didn't work. They tried piggy-back starters, which was almost forward-thinking, considering how baseball started experimenting with openers and Johnny Wholestaff games shortly after. Didn't work.

Then the Rockies realized that the money-in-the-banana-stand theory of baseball actually was in the bullpen, so they pumped a whole mess of money into name-brand relievers at retail prices.

Didn't work.

So, congratulations, you're the GM of the Rockies. You get to build this team. First thing you have to do is, uh, build this team. To do that, you'll need to come up with a strategy.

I have an idea. Free of charge. Build the entire team out of fastball-first starters. Breaking balls don't spin as much in the low air resistance of Denver, so build a team of pitchers who can throw a fastball three-quarters of the time and be successful. That way, the other (dumb) teams are coming in and throwing breaking balls like they always do, and you (smart) have a rotation of pitchers who don't need bendy pitches. Lance Lynn just had one of the best pitching seasons in Rangers history throwing a fastball 71.4 percent of the time, for example.

Great. Sold. Here are the 10 starting pitchers who threw the fastball most often in 2019:

- Lance Lynn
- Brad Keller
- Julio Teheran
- Mike Soroka
- Kyle Hendricks
- José Quintana
- Dakota Hudson
- Walker Buehler
- Noah Syndergaard
- Zack Wheeler

Here's the part where I guess you're supposed to smack Jeff Bridich on the butt and say, "Go get 'em!"

Except those pitchers aren't exactly available, at least not all of them. And, really, once you get past Lynn, it's not like the other pitchers are that extreme. They're almost closer to 30th place in fastball percentage than first.

Got it. So maybe the plan should be for the Rockies to develop their own pitchers. When they won the pennant in 2007, it was with the help of Jeff Francis (1st-round draft pick), Aaron Cook (2nd round) and Ubaldo Jiménez (international free agent).

Except a team should…*always* develop their own pitchers, if possible? They're cheaper, and they're more likely to have their best seasons while under team control. This is a strategy for all 30 teams, not some sort of Coors-buster. Besides, the current iteration of the Rockies is already doing this. When they made the postseason in 2018, it was because they had a rotation filled with homegrown pitchers having tremendous seasons.

Then the pitchers got all squirrely and weird and hurt. As pitchers do. There's at least proof that pitching-first teams will work in Denver, especially with homegrown pitchers who spend their entire minor-league development time adjusting to altitude, though. So far, it's been the franchise's only path to success.

This also highlights the inherent disadvantage the Rockies face, though. Other teams can slap a free agent starter at the back of their rotation for cheap. Or they can go big and allocate a chunk of their payroll for an ace-type free agent starter. Even if those pitchers would consider the Rockies, it's not like anyone would feel especially confident when they're acquired. You want to be excited about the pitchers acquired for millions of dollars, not scrunch up like a human shrug emoji and wait a few months for evidence. So the Rockies are forced to focus on a development-first staff, without fail and regardless of circumstances, which is like forcing the Diamondbacks to ignore left-handed hitters entirely. The Diamondbacks could still find success with an entirely right-handed lineup, sure, but the disadvantage would be immense.

Then, even when there's a thriving, homegrown pitching staff in place, there's the problem of the Coors hangover effect, which is unmistakable and absolutely horrifying. Rockies hitters hit far worse on the road than their talent level suggests they should. This was true in 2019, it was true in 2009, and it was true in 1999. It'll almost certainly be true in 2029.

tOPS+ is a stat that measures the difference between a team's splits, which means you can use it to measure the difference between the Rockies at home and on the road. Here are the 15 worst road tOPS+ marks in baseball history, courtesy of Baseball-Reference:

Rank	Team	Year	Road tOPS+
1	Rockies	1996	59
2	Rockies	2014	66
3	Rockies	2000	69
4	Rockies	2002	70
T5	Phillies	1932	72
T5	Rockies	1995	72
T5	Rockies	1999	72
T8	Rockies	2010	73
T8	Rockies	2012	73
T10	Rockies	1993	74
T10	Rockies	2019	74
12	Rockies	2015	75
T13	Red Sox	1950	76
T13	Red Sox	1955	76
T13	Rockies	2001	76

Again, that's baseball history. Twelve out of the 15 teams with the lowest road tOPS+ all-time are Rockies teams. Before you bring up Coors Field, note that tOPS+ is park adjusted. Even after adjusting for the boost of thin air, the Rockies are especially awful on the road, every year. If you want to use raw OPS, the Rockies still have three of the 10 worst road OPS since 1993 (when they entered the league.) They have six of the 20 worst. That's out of a pool of 800 possible seasons.

So now you have to grow your own pitchers, and you'll also have to figure out how to help your hitters acclimate to sea level for every road trip. Uh, hyperbaric chambers? I don't even know what those are, but I think I remember them from a movie. Maybe there are, uh, you know, *brain implants* that could help the hitters recognize the sharper breaking balls on the road sooner. It's like that famous maxim that neuroscientists use all the time, "Cybernetic implants are the humidor of the brain." Or, no, maybe some sort of virtual reality program that helps rewire the brains of Rockies hitters, that's the ticket.

Also, don't forget about figuring out baseball. You'll have to figure out the game of baseball while doing all of these experiments. It's still extremely hard for the normal teams to figure out baseball, remember.

This, all of this, is why the Rockies have won 90 games or more just three times in 27 seasons. It's why they've finished over .500 just eight times. It's why they've never won a division title. And danged if there's an accessible answer to be found.

In the end, fixing the Rockies isn't as simple as using piggyback starters or building the whole airplane out of expensive relievers, and it never was. The real solution is something totally outlandish, whether it's the aid of a technology that hasn't been invented yet, or MLB somehow putting their thumb on the scale to help them out. If they're wholly reliant on homegrown pitching, how's about an extra draft pick or three? They give extra draft picks to the freaking Cardinals, for crying out loud, just because nobody wants to adjust for the difference between "small market" and "established brand that sweeps across huge swaths of the Midwest," so why not boost their chances of getting another Francis or Freeland?

That'll never happen, of course, so the Rockies will have to juggle more chainsaws than the other 29 teams, and they'll fail more often than they'll succeed. The franchise will be at a crossroads soon, with Trevor Story and Jon Gray being free agents after the 2021 season (and Nolan Arenado able to opt out of his contract), so if the front office and ownership group haven't discussed strip-mining the team for prospects yet, they will soon.

At the same time, their 2020 season shouldn't be so hopeless. If you want to fix *those* Rockies, fix Kyle Freeland. Keep developing Gray. Hope for German Márquez to become the Cy Young contender he absolutely can be. And, sweet mercy, get some hitters around Arenado, Story and Charlie Blackmon. If you can't sign pitchers, at least throw the door open for the hitters, and don't be a bunch of weirdos and sign a shortstop to play first base this time. There is still a window here. Even after the dreadful 2019 season, there is still a window worth chasing.

Because if that window shuts, the Rockies will be at the bottom of the mountain range, rubble all around them. They'll look to the left and see a team with carabiners and Prusik cords. They'll look to the right and see a team with an ice axe, a harness, and an assortment of ropes. Then they'll have to dust themselves off, armed with nothing but a spork and some superglue, and start climbing that mountain all over again.

—Grant Brisbee is an author at The Athletic Bay Area.

Part 2: Player Analysis

Colorado Rockies 2020

PLAYER COMMENTS WITH GRAPHS

Yonder Alonso 1B
Born: 04/08/87 Age: 33 Bats: L Throws: R
Height: 6'1" Weight: 230 Origin: Round 1, 2008 Draft (#7 overall)

YEAR	TEAM	LVL	AGE	PA	R	2B	3B	HR	RBI	BB	K	SB	CS	AVG/OBP/SLG
2017	OAK	MLB	30	371	52	17	0	22	49	50	88	1	0	.266/.369/.527
2017	SEA	MLB	30	150	20	5	0	6	18	18	30	1	0	.265/.353/.439
2018	CLE	MLB	31	574	64	19	0	23	83	51	123	0	0	.250/.317/.421
2019	ABQ	AAA	32	38	7	3	1	2	12	5	6	0	0	.419/.500/.774
2019	COL	MLB	32	84	11	7	0	3	10	10	17	0	0	.260/.357/.479
2019	CHA	MLB	32	251	23	6	0	7	27	29	53	0	1	.178/.275/.301
2020	COL	MLB	33	251	26	11	0	8	28	26	52	1	1	.225/.310/.382

Comparables: Paul Konerko, Torii Hunter, Michael Cuddyer

As revolutions go, Alonso's personal launch angle overhaul has proven to be more 1979 Nicaragua than 1789 France. Explosive initial change gave way to mediocrity that looked awfully like the old version, with a slightly different batted-ball mix producing essentially the same results. If 2018 was evidence that nothing had really changed, 2019 suggested that the new Alonso might be worse than the old. A disastrous half-season with the White Sox saw him booted out of Chicago in favor of...well, anyone who could swing a bat, including most of their catchers and Matt Skole. The Rockies picked him up and used him tremendously sparingly, with starts in just 10 of his 54 games. The line improved a great deal in Colorado, albeit only to his typical career league-average mark. Alonso needs another transformation if he's going to convince teams he isn't just following the path of many revolutionaries before him: clinging on to his position long after it's clear a change is needed.

YEAR	TEAM	LVL	AGE	PA	DRC+	VORP	BABIP	BRR	FRAA	WARP
2017	OAK	MLB	30	371	123	17.8	.301	-0.2	1B(96): -2.7	1.3
2017	SEA	MLB	30	150	125	2.3	.302	-0.1	1B(39): -2.8	0.4
2018	CLE	MLB	31	574	96	7.6	.283	1.1	1B(138): -0.6	0.6
2019	ABQ	AAA	32	38	145	4.1	.458	-1.5	1B(8): -0.2	0.1
2019	COL	MLB	32	84	102	2.2	.302	0.3	1B(11): -1.1	0.1
2019	CHA	MLB	32	251	79	-3.0	.199	0.1	1B(21): -0.1	-0.3
2020	COL	MLB	33	251	84	3.0	.261	0.1	1B -2	0.1

Yonder Alonso, continued

Batted Ball Distribution

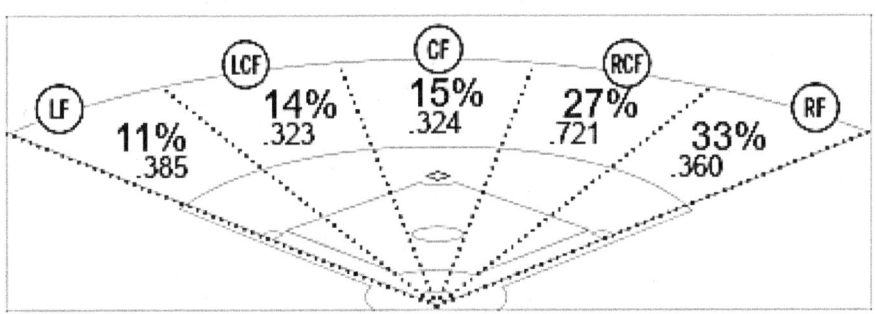

Strike Zone vs LHP   **Strike Zone vs RHP**

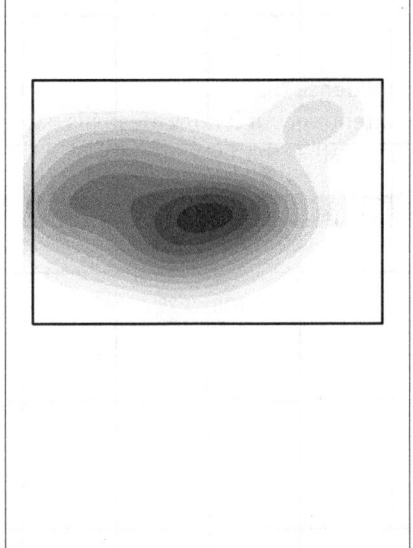

Nolan Arenado 3B

Born: 04/16/91   Age: 29   Bats: R   Throws: R
Height: 6'2"   Weight: 215   Origin: Round 2, 2009 Draft (#59 overall)

YEAR	TEAM	LVL	AGE	PA	R	2B	3B	HR	RBI	BB	K	SB	CS	AVG/OBP/SLG
2017	COL	MLB	26	680	100	43	7	37	130	62	106	3	2	.309/.373/.586
2018	COL	MLB	27	673	104	38	2	38	110	73	122	2	2	.297/.374/.561
2019	COL	MLB	28	662	102	31	2	41	118	62	93	3	2	.315/.379/.583
2020	COL	MLB	29	630	93	35	4	38	110	55	100	4	2	.308/.373/.587

Comparables: Aramis Ramirez, Adrián Beltré, Lonnie Chisenhall

The Rockies rewarded Arenado for his stellar production with an eight-year, $260 million deal. He repaid them in kind with a fifth-straight season of at least six WARP, 660 plate appearances, 127 DRC+ and 37 homers. It had little impact on a team that utterly failed to build on its trip to the playoffs. Arenado may grow impatient without significant team improvement, if he isn't already. Impatience was certainly in evidence at the plate, despite the consistent slash line. Arenado saw his fewest pitches per plate appearance since 2015 and swung at a career-high 35.4 percent of first pitches. Fortunately, Jeff Bridich insisted on inserting an opt-out in that deal after 2021. That may not fill Arenado with confidence that the front office will maneuver their way back into playoff contention, but it does mean his patience will only have to last another two years rather than seven.

YEAR	TEAM	LVL	AGE	PA	DRC+	VORP	BABIP	BRR	FRAA	WARP
2017	COL	MLB	26	680	136	61.5	.320	-0.5	3B(157): 5.0	6.0
2018	COL	MLB	27	673	138	48.3	.314	-2.9	3B(152): 9.1	6.2
2019	COL	MLB	28	662	136	56.8	.312	2.0	3B(154): 14.2	7.1
2020	COL	MLB	29	630	133	41.8	.318	-0.3	3B 6	5.0

Nolan Arenado, continued

Batted Ball Distribution

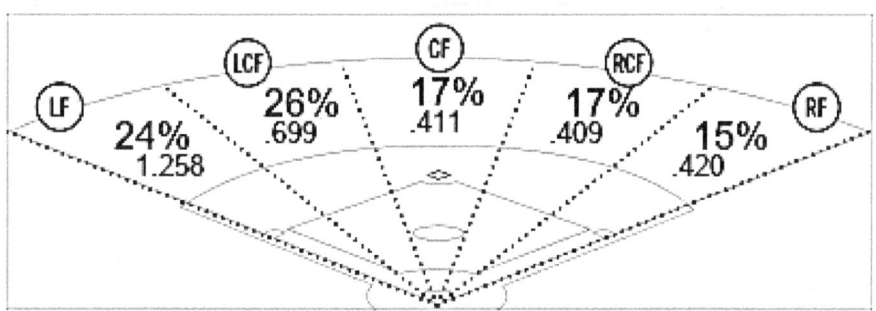

Strike Zone vs LHP   **Strike Zone vs RHP**

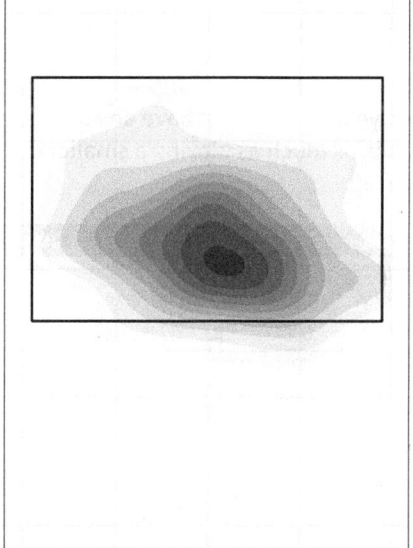

Charlie Blackmon RF

Born: 07/01/86   Age: 33   Bats: L   Throws: L
Height: 6'3"   Weight: 220   Origin: Round 2, 2008 Draft (#72 overall)

YEAR	TEAM	LVL	AGE	PA	R	2B	3B	HR	RBI	BB	K	SB	CS	AVG/OBP/SLG
2017	COL	MLB	30	725	137	35	14	37	104	65	135	14	10	.331/.399/.601
2018	COL	MLB	31	696	119	31	7	29	70	59	134	12	4	.291/.358/.502
2019	COL	MLB	32	634	112	42	7	32	86	40	104	2	5	.314/.364/.576
2020	COL	MLB	34	595	78	33	7	26	88	41	109	16	7	.301/.360/.530

Comparables: Alex Rios, Jon Jay, Denard Span

Concerns that Blackmon's contract extension might have been poorly-timed were assuaged with a performance that was close to, if not quite at, Blackmon's offensive peak at the plate. Colorado addressed his disastrous defensive 2018 in center field by fully embracing a logical move to a corner, with one hundred percent of Blackmon's defensive innings coming in right field. Unfortunately, it seems that Chuck's Nazty-ness with the glove has outpaced that move as he still rated as one of the worst defensive outfielders in the game, even at the easier position. Blackmon no longer needs to worry about what he'll do after leaving Coors, since his extension keeps him there through 2023 if he so desires. Given that he now has the largest home-road OPS split of any player in history, the 33-year-old may not have any interest in finding out how he'd fare with another club, as much as playing a smaller outfield would compensate for his loss of speed.

YEAR	TEAM	LVL	AGE	PA	DRC+	VORP	BABIP	BRR	FRAA	WARP
2017	COL	MLB	30	725	144	77.3	.371	1.6	CF(158): -0.1	6.7
2018	COL	MLB	31	696	123	38.4	.329	-0.6	CF(151): -21.7	2.1
2019	COL	MLB	32	634	129	39.1	.334	0.4	RF(135): -8.8	3.0
2020	COL	MLB	34	595	123	31.1	.337	0.3	RF -6	2.6

Charlie Blackmon, continued

Batted Ball Distribution

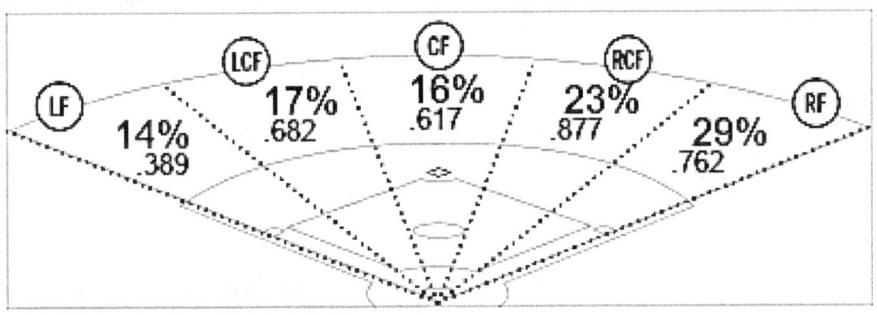

Strike Zone vs LHP   **Strike Zone vs RHP**

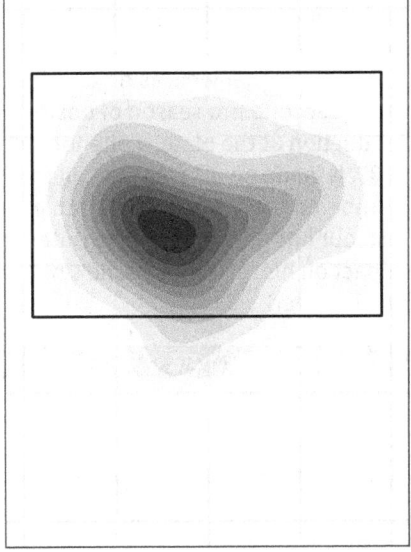

Colorado Rockies 2020

Drew Butera C

Born: 08/09/83 Age: 36 Bats: R Throws: R
Height: 6'1" Weight: 205 Origin: Round 5, 2005 Draft (#149 overall)

YEAR	TEAM	LVL	AGE	PA	R	2B	3B	HR	RBI	BB	K	SB	CS	AVG/OBP/SLG
2017	KCA	MLB	33	177	18	4	1	3	14	12	41	0	0	.227/.284/.319
2018	KCA	MLB	34	166	11	9	0	2	18	13	37	0	0	.188/.259/.289
2018	COL	MLB	34	16	2	0	0	1	3	2	2	0	0	.214/.313/.429
2019	ABQ	AAA	35	262	38	16	2	9	40	33	55	2	0	.300/.389/.511
2019	COL	MLB	35	49	6	3	0	0	3	4	14	0	0	.163/.229/.233
2020	COL	MLB	36	35	3	2	0	1	4	3	10	0	0	.232/.300/.378

Comparables: Chris Cannizzaro, Matt Treanor, Jim Sundberg

YEAR	TEAM	P. COUNT	FRM RUNS	BLK RUNS	THRW RUNS	TOT RUNS
2017	KCA	7350	-4.2	2.0	-0.2	-3.0
2018	KCA	6521	-6.4	0.0	-0.2	-6.8
2018	COL	730	-0.7	-0.1	0.0	-0.9
2019	ABQ	9577	-7.5	-0.2	0.4	-7.5
2019	COL	1969	-1.3	1.2	0.0	-0.1
2020	COL	1750	-1.1	0.3	0.1	-0.7

Butera has made a career out of hanging on to a major-league spot as a backup catcher. His tenuous grip on a job at the highest level started to slip in 2019 as he was forced to don the tools of ignorance in the minor leagues for the first time in six years. Triple-A suited him rather well, as he supplied just his second pro season of positive production at the plate, a phenomenon not seen since his stint at High-A in 2007. It made no difference at all to his big-league numbers when he finally clambered back onto the 40-man in September, with the 35-year-old recording just four hits all month. While Butera's batting performance has never had much impact on his roster status, he's not going to be able to keep clinging on for much longer.

YEAR	TEAM	LVL	AGE	PA	DRC+	VORP	BABIP	BRR	FRAA	WARP
2017	KCA	MLB	33	177	84	1.3	.286	-0.1	C(74): -3.4, 1B(4): -0.2	0.2
2018	KCA	MLB	34	166	80	-0.4	.232	1.2	C(48): -6.9, 1B(2): 0.9	-0.1
2018	COL	MLB	34	16	78	0.5	.182	0.1	C(6): -0.9, 1B(4): 0.0	-0.1
2019	ABQ	AAA	35	262	108	17.5	.356	0.3	C(64): -5.7	1.1
2019	COL	MLB	35	49	63	0.0	.233	0.5	C(14): 0.2, 1B(3): 0.0	0.1
2020	COL	MLB	36	35	69	0.3	.304	0.1	C -1	0.0

Drew Butera, continued

Batted Ball Distribution

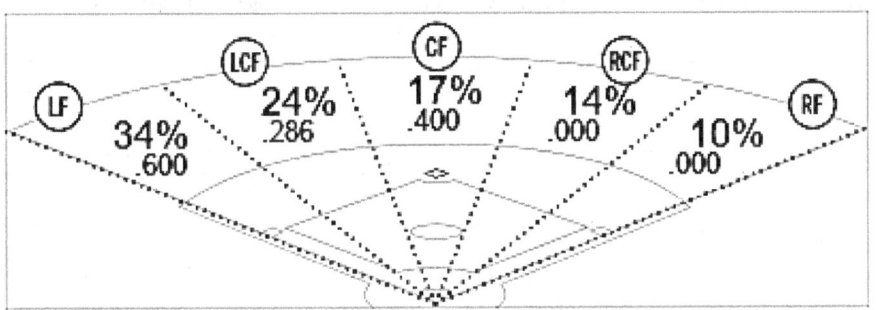

Strike Zone vs LHP

Strike Zone vs RHP

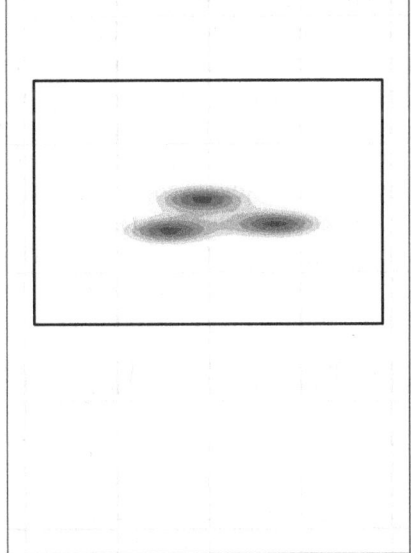

Colorado Rockies 2020

David Dahl OF
Born: 04/01/94   Age: 26   Bats: L   Throws: R
Height: 6'2"   Weight: 200   Origin: Round 1, 2012 Draft (#10 overall)

YEAR	TEAM	LVL	AGE	PA	R	2B	3B	HR	RBI	BB	K	SB	CS	AVG/OBP/SLG
2017	ABQ	AAA	23	74	12	2	2	2	14	3	17	1	1	.243/.274/.414
2018	ABQ	AAA	24	78	7	7	0	2	9	1	19	1	0	.286/.295/.455
2018	COL	MLB	24	271	31	11	3	16	48	19	68	5	3	.273/.325/.534
2019	COL	MLB	25	413	67	28	5	15	61	28	110	4	4	.302/.353/.524
2020	COL	MLB	26	462	53	22	5	18	61	27	125	12	4	.271/.317/.467

Comparables: Eddie Rosario, Junior Lake, Jake Marisnick

It was going so well for Dahl in his battle with the injury-prone tag. Even with a slight core issue, Dahl appeared in 100 of the first 110 contests, making his first All-Star game in the process. Then disaster struck once again: In an August 2nd game against the Giants, the 25-year-old was tracking down a line drive when his foot got caught in the Coors Field turf and his ankle moved in ways it's certainly not supposed to. Dahl made the catch; he also missed the remaining two months of the season with a high ankle sprain. He therefore once again managed to fuel the injury-prone narrative with a different ailment from those that had sidelined him previously. It's theoretically encouraging that Dahl doesn't have a chronic problem, and yet with every passing year it's becoming harder to shake the notion that he simply can't play every day without sustaining an injury at some point. This was the first time he'd reached triple-digit games since 2014 and also one of his most mediocre offensive performances, by DRC's reckoning. One can argue that a fully healthy season will also lead to better production with the bat. Let's hope that argument doesn't remain purely theoretical.

YEAR	TEAM	LVL	AGE	PA	DRC+	VORP	BABIP	BRR	FRAA	WARP
2017	ABQ	AAA	23	74	56	0.4	.294	0.7	CF(6): -0.3, LF(6): -0.2	-0.2
2018	ABQ	AAA	24	78	85	-0.4	.357	-0.6	RF(6): 0.2, CF(6): 0.4	0.2
2018	COL	MLB	24	271	112	8.7	.311	-1.3	LF(34): 2.9, RF(30): -1.4	1.1
2019	COL	MLB	25	413	103	14.4	.386	2.1	CF(40): 1.3, LF(39): 0.2	1.3
2020	COL	MLB	26	462	96	12.6	.344	0.9	CF 0, LF 3	1.6

David Dahl, continued

Batted Ball Distribution

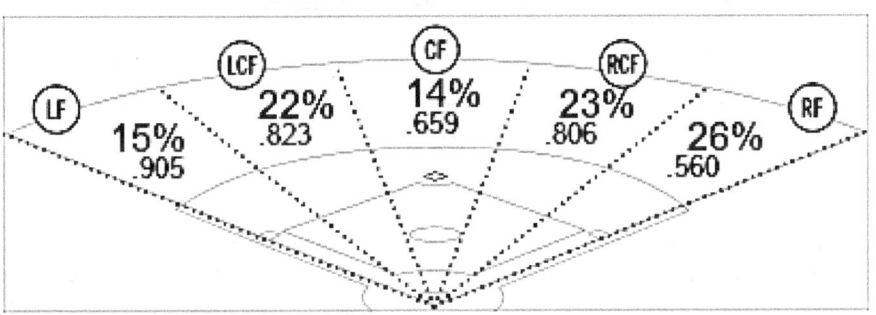

Strike Zone vs LHP   **Strike Zone vs RHP**

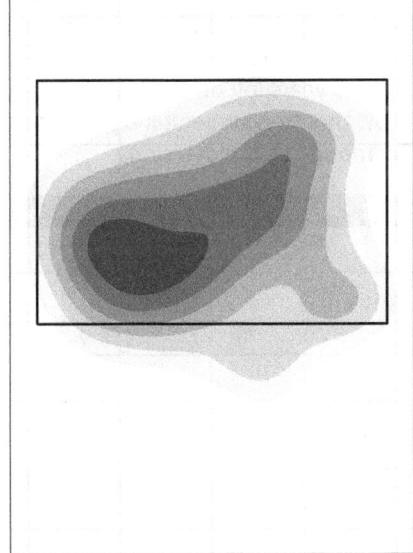

Ian Desmond OF

Born: 09/20/85 Age: 34 Bats: R Throws: R
Height: 6'3" Weight: 220 Origin: Round 3, 2004 Draft (#84 overall)

YEAR	TEAM	LVL	AGE	PA	R	2B	3B	HR	RBI	BB	K	SB	CS	AVG/OBP/SLG
2017	COL	MLB	31	373	47	11	1	7	40	24	87	15	4	.274/.326/.375
2018	COL	MLB	32	619	82	21	8	22	88	53	146	20	6	.236/.307/.422
2019	COL	MLB	33	482	64	31	4	20	65	34	119	3	3	.255/.310/.479
2020	COL	MLB	34	336	37	14	3	12	41	24	91	8	3	.245/.305/.424

Comparables: Jhonny Peralta, Troy Tulowitzki, Alex Gonzalez

Desmond's arrival in Colorado three years ago coincided with their most competitive period in a decade. It's unfortunate, then, that he has done virtually nothing to contribute to that success. The Rockies moved away from the baffling first base plan in 2019 with an even more baffling move up the defensive spectrum to center field. While FRAA is a little kinder to Desmond than other defensive metrics, that only serves to make him around replacement-level rather than clearly below when combined with his thoroughly subpar performance at the plate. After almost 400 games of futility, the team has relented a little: Desmond only appeared in 140 contests rather than 160. There are two years left on his deal, so there's plenty more time for the Rockies to show that they understand sunk cost better than we understand any of their Desmond-related decisions.

YEAR	TEAM	LVL	AGE	PA	DRC+	VORP	BABIP	BRR	FRAA	WARP
2017	COL	MLB	31	373	74	3.3	.345	2.7	LF(66): -2.8, 1B(27): -2.5	-0.6
2018	COL	MLB	32	619	90	4.8	.279	0.8	1B(138): -2.6, LF(18): 0.8	0.2
2019	COL	MLB	33	482	86	7.3	.304	0.4	CF(74): -12.8, LF(44): -2.9	-0.8
2020	COL	MLB	34	336	78	2.5	.309	0.6	CF -5, LF -1	-0.3

Ian Desmond, continued

Batted Ball Distribution

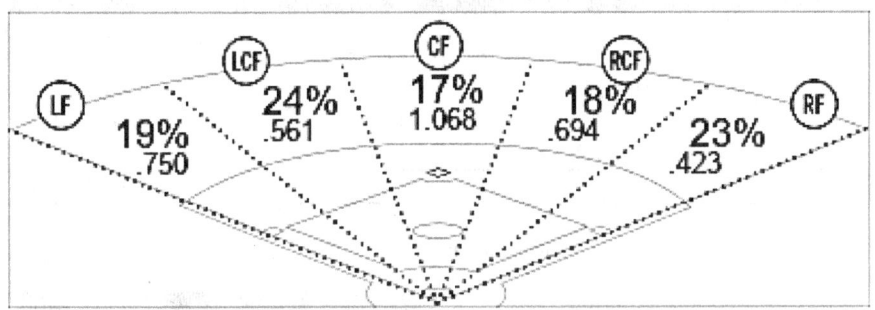

Strike Zone vs LHP   Strike Zone vs RHP

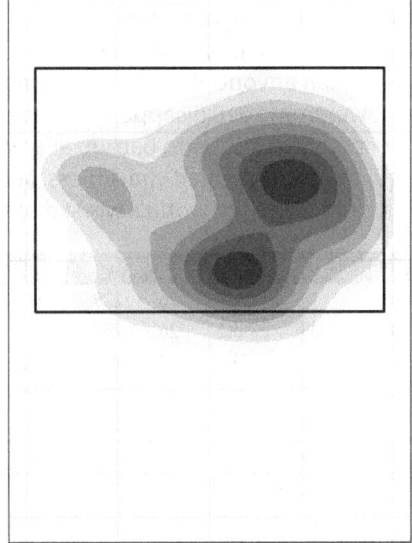

Elias Díaz   C

Born: 11/17/90   Age: 29   Bats: R   Throws: R
Height: 6'1"   Weight: 220   Origin: International Free Agent, 2008

YEAR	TEAM	LVL	AGE	PA	R	2B	3B	HR	RBI	BB	K	SB	CS	AVG/OBP/SLG
2017	IND	AAA	26	229	19	10	0	2	27	9	36	3	0	.266/.298/.339
2017	PIT	MLB	26	200	18	14	0	1	19	11	38	1	0	.223/.265/.314
2018	PIT	MLB	27	277	33	12	0	10	34	21	40	0	1	.286/.339/.452
2019	IND	AAA	28	30	5	3	0	0	4	1	5	0	0	.414/.433/.517
2019	PIT	MLB	28	332	31	14	0	2	28	23	56	0	0	.241/.296/.307
2020	PIT	MLB	29	251	22	12	0	4	24	17	47	1	1	.240/.295/.350

Comparables: Carlos Pèrez, Steve Clevenger, Yonder Alonso

George Carlin once said that somebody has to be the world's worst doctor, and that someone has an appointment with them tomorrow. Likewise, someone has to be the worst catcher in framing runs, and it happened to be Díaz—nearly four runs worse than anyone else. His wellspring of power from 2018 disappeared, and in the process his outlook downgraded from potential starter to backup at best. He did begin the season on the injured list with an unspecified viral illness. Maybe his poor effort can be blamed on office time with the world's worst doctor?

YEAR	TEAM	P. COUNT	FRM RUNS	BLK RUNS	THRW RUNS	TOT RUNS
2017	IND	7000	1.3	-0.4	0.8	1.2
2017	PIT	6832	-5.1	-0.7	0.2	-6.2
2018	PIT	9111	-1.2	-2.0	0.1	-3.2
2019	PIT	12591	-14.4	0.1	-0.1	-14.4
2020	PIT	9391	-4.6	-0.3	-0.3	-5.2

YEAR	TEAM	LVL	AGE	PA	DRC+	VORP	BABIP	BRR	FRAA	WARP
2017	IND	AAA	26	229	88	2.1	.311	-1.2	C(50): 6.3	1.2
2017	PIT	MLB	26	200	62	-4.8	.273	-0.9	C(55): -3.8	-0.4
2018	PIT	MLB	27	277	113	21.2	.302	0.5	C(70): 0.6	1.9
2019	IND	AAA	28	30	118	3.7	.500	0.0	C(6): 0.7	0.2
2019	PIT	MLB	28	332	73	5.6	.286	1.3	C(96): -11.0	-0.4
2020	PIT	MLB	29	251	72	-0.9	.285	0.3	C -2	-0.3

Elias Díaz, continued

Batted Ball Distribution

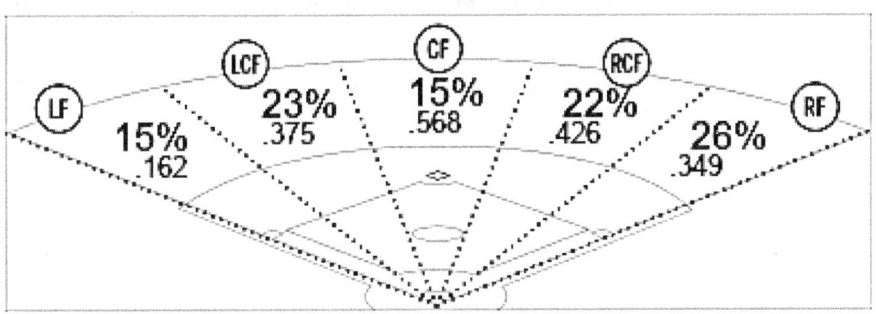

Strike Zone vs LHP   **Strike Zone vs RHP**

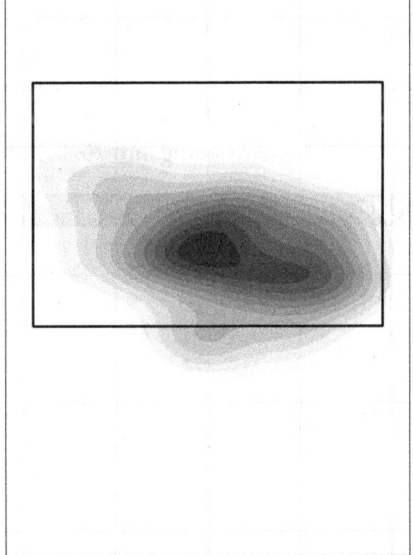

Garrett Hampson 2B

Born: 10/10/94 Age: 25 Bats: R Throws: R
Height: 5'11" Weight: 188 Origin: Round 3, 2016 Draft (#81 overall)

YEAR	TEAM	LVL	AGE	PA	R	2B	3B	HR	RBI	BB	K	SB	CS	AVG/OBP/SLG
2017	LNC	A+	22	603	113	24	12	8	70	56	77	51	14	.326/.387/.462
2018	HFD	AA	23	172	28	8	2	4	15	21	17	19	1	.304/.391/.466
2018	ABQ	AAA	23	332	53	17	4	6	25	30	58	17	4	.314/.377/.459
2018	COL	MLB	23	48	3	3	1	0	4	7	12	2	0	.275/.396/.400
2019	ABQ	AAA	24	117	15	9	1	2	9	5	25	7	2	.266/.310/.422
2019	COL	MLB	24	327	40	9	4	8	27	24	88	15	3	.247/.302/.385
2020	COL	MLB	25	350	35	14	5	7	35	26	90	17	4	.256/.314/.392

Comparables: Roy McMillan, Joe Demaestri, Pete Runnels

What looked like a complicated path to playing time for the speedy Hampson turned into a golden chance right out of the blocks as both Ryan McMahon and Daniel Murphy got hurt inside the first 10 games of the season. Hampson didn't run, either with the opportunity or on the basepaths, stumbling to one of the worst offensive months in Rockies history. That false start followed by several more disqualified him from a regular role until the season's final month. Hampson made up for lost time with a .903 OPS in September, dazzling on the bases and adding five homers for good measure. The complicated playing time situation remains going into 2020, but it's a marathon, not a sprint.

YEAR	TEAM	LVL	AGE	PA	DRC+	VORP	BABIP	BRR	FRAA	WARP
2017	LNC	A+	22	603	128	41.5	.364	7.5	2B(71): -0.4, SS(56): 7.3	5.4
2018	HFD	AA	23	172	136	18.7	.323	3.5	SS(18): 0.4, 2B(17): 1.7	1.9
2018	ABQ	AAA	23	332	110	16.9	.372	0.9	2B(44): -0.1, SS(23): -2.3	1.6
2018	COL	MLB	23	48	81	3.6	.393	1.1	SS(8): 0.2, 2B(7): 0.6	0.2
2019	ABQ	AAA	24	117	63	0.8	.329	1.0	2B(15): 0.3, SS(10): -1.5	-0.1
2019	COL	MLB	24	327	71	-0.5	.322	3.5	2B(50): -1.1, CF(31): -0.8	0.1
2020	COL	MLB	25	350	73	3.6	.337	2.3	CF 0, 2B 0	0.4

Garrett Hampson, continued

Batted Ball Distribution

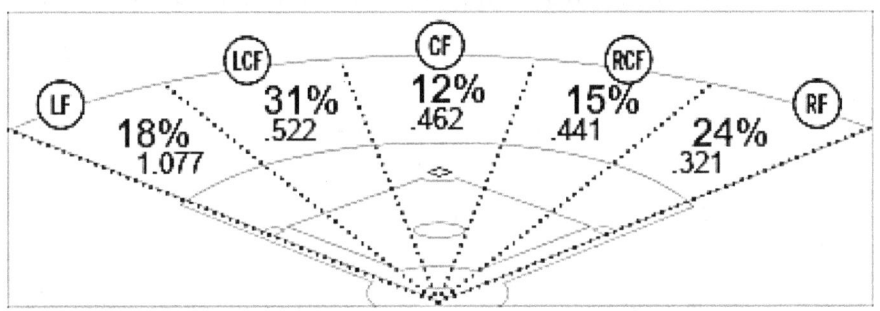

| Strike Zone vs LHP | Strike Zone vs RHP |

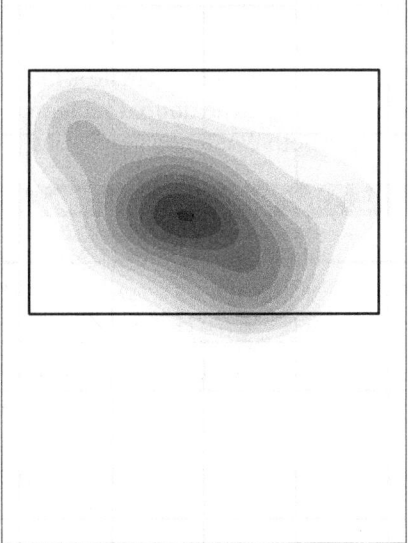

Colorado Rockies 2020

Sam Hilliard OF

Born: 02/21/94 Age: 26 Bats: L Throws: L
Height: 6'5" Weight: 238 Origin: Round 15, 2015 Draft (#437 overall)

YEAR	TEAM	LVL	AGE	PA	R	2B	3B	HR	RBI	BB	K	SB	CS	AVG/OBP/SLG
2017	LNC	A+	23	597	95	23	7	21	92	50	154	37	17	.300/.360/.487
2018	HFD	AA	24	484	58	22	3	9	40	41	151	23	14	.262/.327/.389
2019	ABQ	AAA	25	559	109	29	7	35	101	54	164	22	5	.262/.335/.558
2019	COL	MLB	25	87	13	4	2	7	13	9	23	2	0	.273/.356/.649
2020	COL	MLB	26	154	16	7	1	5	17	12	51	4	2	.222/.285/.388

Comparables: Jared Walsh, Aristides Aquino, Donald Lutz

No Hilliard had ever made the majors before Sam—not unless one includes 1930s infielder Meredith Hilliard Hopkins, who hardly counts, not least because he went by Marty. Sam's monster raw power showed up in a big way in 2019, with a near-.300 ISO at Albuquerque, and then a mark over 80 points higher in his big-league debut. Questions still need to be answered about his ability to regularly get that power into games given his pitch recognition issues and accompanying high strikeout rate. His platoon problems seem to have faded, however, and if he can hit for remotely this much power, then he won't need to keep playing center, where he is rather stretched. Even for Hilliard fun fact sticklers, there's no doubt that Sam is the best of all time: he has already passed Marty in both WARP and home runs, with barely a sixth of the playing time.

YEAR	TEAM	LVL	AGE	PA	DRC+	VORP	BABIP	BRR	FRAA	WARP
2017	LNC	A+	23	597	121	25.1	.384	3.9	RF(85): 6.6, LF(30): 5.1	4.1
2018	HFD	AA	24	484	97	9.1	.379	0.3	RF(70): 3.5, LF(29): -1.8	1.1
2019	ABQ	AAA	25	559	98	17.0	.316	0.5	RF(82): -0.2, CF(33): 5.2	1.8
2019	COL	MLB	25	87	109	3.8	.298	0.7	CF(17): 0.6, RF(6): 1.7	0.5
2020	COL	MLB	26	154	70	-0.8	.311	0.4	CF 2, LF 0	0.1

Sam Hilliard, continued

Batted Ball Distribution

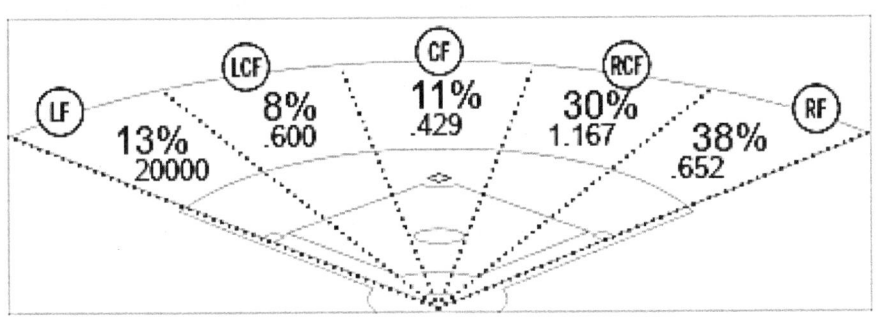

Strike Zone vs LHP **Strike Zone vs RHP**

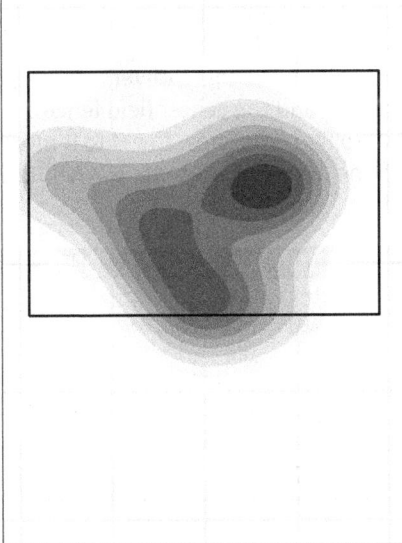

Ryan McMahon INF

Born: 12/14/94 Age: 25 Bats: L Throws: R
Height: 6'2" Weight: 208 Origin: Round 2, 2013 Draft (#42 overall)

YEAR	TEAM	LVL	AGE	PA	R	2B	3B	HR	RBI	BB	K	SB	CS	AVG/OBP/SLG
2017	HFD	AA	22	205	28	16	2	6	32	20	39	7	0	.326/.390/.536
2017	ABQ	AAA	22	314	46	23	2	14	56	21	53	4	3	.374/.411/.612
2017	COL	MLB	22	24	2	1	0	0	1	5	5	0	0	.158/.333/.211
2018	ABQ	AAA	23	242	40	15	3	11	48	15	61	3	2	.290/.339/.531
2018	COL	MLB	23	202	17	9	1	5	19	18	64	1	0	.232/.307/.376
2019	COL	MLB	24	539	70	22	1	24	83	56	160	5	1	.250/.329/.450
2020	COL	MLB	25	539	63	21	2	22	70	48	163	5	3	.247/.319/.434

Comparables: Tommy Brown, Byron Buxton, Clint Frazier

The Rockies *almost* committed to McMahon as an everyday option, employing him as their primary second baseman with a smattering of appearances at both infield corners. He played the keystone reasonably well while improving, if not excelling, with the bat. There are still a lot of whiffs in this profile, and McMahon hasn't yet been able to find the level of power that would make them palatable. Sure, the loud contact is there, but too much of it sends the ball into the ground rather than the thin Denver air. Every now and then, McMahon launches one way beyond the center field fence to remind us the ability is there. Now he just has to figure out how to get to it more often. He might need to in order to fight off the queue of alternatives waiting to take infield time away from him. from him.

YEAR	TEAM	LVL	AGE	PA	DRC+	VORP	BABIP	BRR	FRAA	WARP
2017	HFD	AA	22	205	141	15.7	.381	0.0	1B(25): 0.4, 2B(15): 2.1	1.7
2017	ABQ	AAA	22	314	150	26.3	.416	-2.9	1B(36): 1.1, 2B(24): 2.4	2.6
2017	COL	MLB	22	24	76	0.3	.214	1.4	1B(7): 0.2, 2B(4): 0.0	0.1
2018	ABQ	AAA	23	242	107	5.6	.353	1.9	1B(43): -1.9, 2B(10): -1.0	0.5
2018	COL	MLB	23	202	74	0.0	.327	0.9	1B(31): -1.1, 3B(17): 0.1	-0.1
2019	COL	MLB	24	539	92	11.6	.323	-0.1	2B(113): 6.9, 3B(22): -0.5	1.7
2020	COL	MLB	25	539	91	15.4	.326	0.5	2B 7, 1B 0	2.3

Ryan McMahon, continued

Batted Ball Distribution

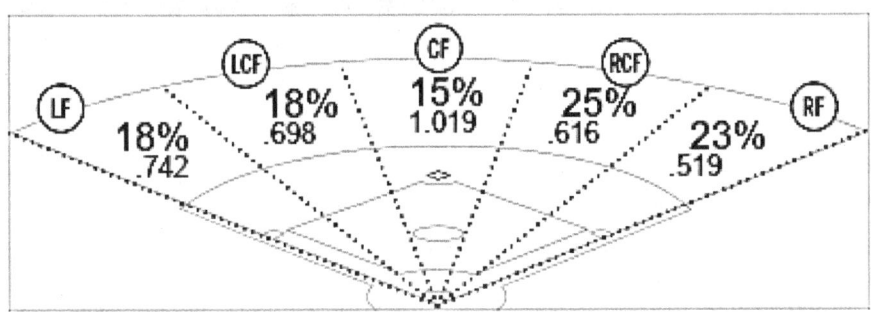

Strike Zone vs LHP   **Strike Zone vs RHP**

Daniel Murphy 1B

Born: 04/01/85   Age: 35   Bats: L   Throws: R
Height: 6'1"   Weight: 221   Origin: Round 13, 2006 Draft (#394 overall)

YEAR	TEAM	LVL	AGE	PA	R	2B	3B	HR	RBI	BB	K	SB	CS	AVG/OBP/SLG
2017	WAS	MLB	32	593	94	43	3	23	93	52	77	2	0	.322/.384/.543
2018	HAR	AA	33	44	8	2	0	2	7	6	4	0	0	.243/.364/.459
2018	WAS	MLB	33	205	17	9	0	6	29	13	17	1	0	.300/.341/.442
2018	CHN	MLB	33	146	23	6	0	6	13	7	23	2	0	.297/.329/.471
2019	COL	MLB	34	478	56	35	1	13	78	32	74	1	1	.279/.328/.452
2020	COL	MLB	35	511	55	30	2	15	61	35	80	3	1	.277/.331/.442

Comparables: Juan Rivera, Elston Howard, Omar Infante

Murphy heading to Coors looked like a batting title waiting to happen. It worked for Justin Morneau and Michael Cuddyer in their mid-thirties. Instead, we got an extremely Mets Murphy line, one that was almost identical to his final year in New York. That's not a good sign given the respective contexts in which those two seasons were played. There were mitigating circumstances. A broken index finger put his season on hold before it even got started and continued to bother him long after he returned. Murphy will get another shot at that batting title in the second year of his deal. It's about time a Rockie won one.

YEAR	TEAM	LVL	AGE	PA	DRC+	VORP	BABIP	BRR	FRAA	WARP
2017	WAS	MLB	32	593	133	51.4	.341	1.2	2B(139): 3.8	4.8
2018	HAR	AA	33	44	121	3.6	.226	0.5	2B(8): -0.6, 1B(2): 0.3	0.2
2018	WAS	MLB	33	205	114	8.3	.302	-1.0	2B(38): -2.9, 1B(14): -0.6	0.4
2018	CHN	MLB	33	146	112	8.1	.318	0.7	2B(33): -1.1	0.6
2019	COL	MLB	34	478	97	6.2	.307	0.0	1B(110): 5.9, 2B(3): 0.4	1.2
2020	COL	MLB	35	511	96	7.4	.307	0.1	1B 5	1.3

Daniel Murphy, continued

Batted Ball Distribution

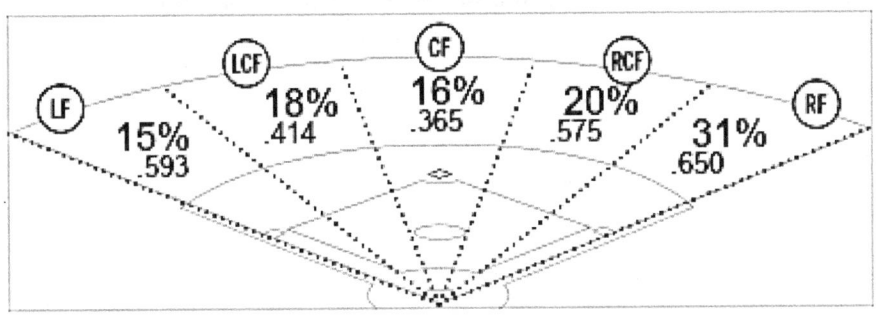

Strike Zone vs LHP   **Strike Zone vs RHP**

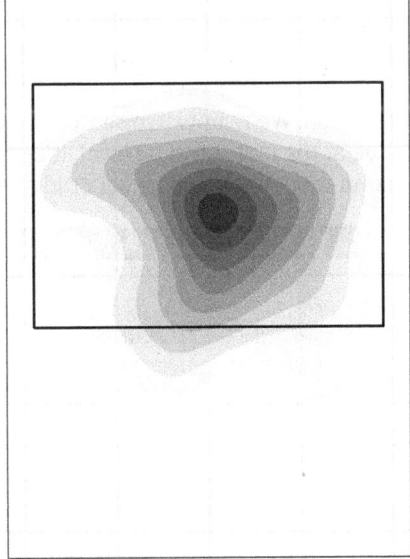

Colorado Rockies 2020

Chris Owings SS

Born: 08/12/91 Age: 28 Bats: R Throws: R
Height: 5'10" Weight: 185 Origin: Round 1, 2009 Draft (#41 overall)

YEAR	TEAM	LVL	AGE	PA	R	2B	3B	HR	RBI	BB	K	SB	CS	AVG/OBP/SLG
2017	ARI	MLB	25	386	41	25	1	12	51	17	87	12	2	.268/.299/.442
2018	RNO	AAA	26	92	15	4	2	1	11	1	17	1	2	.286/.293/.407
2018	ARI	MLB	26	309	34	15	0	4	22	24	75	11	4	.206/.272/.302
2019	PAW	AAA	27	183	26	11	0	11	34	15	50	6	4	.325/.385/.595
2019	KCA	MLB	27	145	9	4	1	2	9	8	55	4	1	.133/.193/.222
2019	BOS	MLB	27	51	4	2	0	1	5	6	23	1	1	.156/.255/.267
2020	BOS	MLB	28	251	21	10	1	5	23	15	81	7	2	.199/.251/.316

Comparables: Alex Gonzalez, Granny Hamner, Leo Cardenas

Excluding the members of the Astros PR department, you'd be hard pressed to find someone who had a worse 2019 than Owings. He wasn't good enough for the 2019 Royals, who finished 12th in the AL in team DRC+. He wasn't good enough for the 2019 Red Sox, who showed about as much life down the stretch as a taxidermied possum. The exhaustive list of hitters who received as many plate appearances as Owings and who performed worse is as follows: Colin Moran, Wellington Castillo, Christin Stewart, John Hicks, Chris Davis and Stevie Wilkerson. We're now two seasons out from Owings providing any semblance of value at the major-league level. It's beginning to look like, just maybe, the Diamondbacks should've kept Didi Gregorius instead.

YEAR	TEAM	LVL	AGE	PA	DRC+	VORP	BABIP	BRR	FRAA	WARP
2017	ARI	MLB	25	386	85	14.5	.318	-0.6	SS(54): 4.2, RF(25): 1.5	1.2
2018	RNO	AAA	26	92	67	-0.6	.342	1.4	2B(10): -0.2, 3B(6): 0.3	0.1
2018	ARI	MLB	26	309	70	-6.2	.265	0.8	RF(43): -1.1, CF(16): 1.2	-0.4
2019	PAW	AAA	27	183	140	22.8	.404	-1.0	SS(18): 0.3, 2B(10): 1.5	1.4
2019	KCA	MLB	27	145	35	-7.2	.205	0.9	2B(13): -1.8, 3B(12): 1.4	-0.7
2019	BOS	MLB	27	51	29	-2.8	.286	-1.0	2B(12): 0.2, SS(7): 0.7	-0.3
2020	BOS	MLB	28	251	48	-9.0	.281	-0.1	SS 1, 2B 0	-0.9

Chris Owings, continued

Batted Ball Distribution

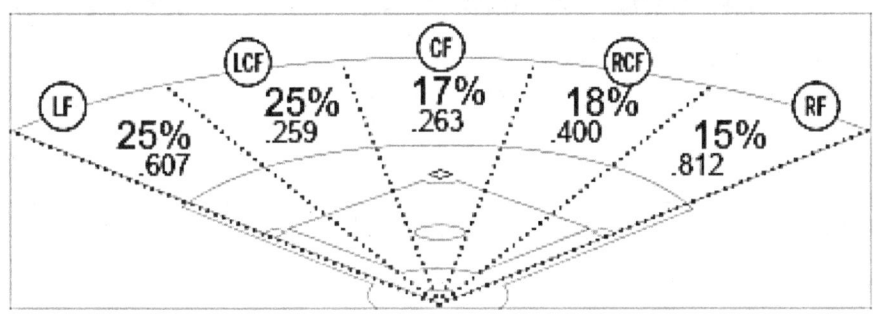

Strike Zone vs LHP **Strike Zone vs RHP**

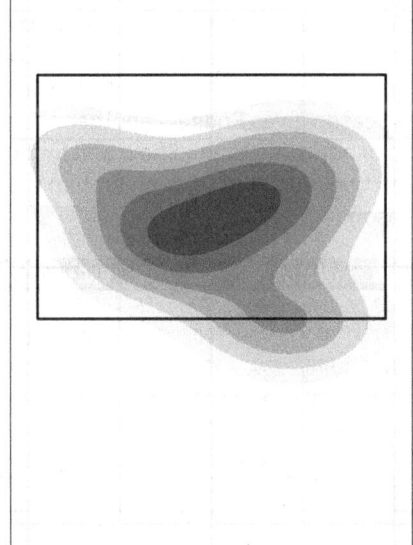

Colorado Rockies 2020

Brendan Rodgers 2B
Born: 08/09/96   Age: 23   Bats: R   Throws: R
Height: 6'0"   Weight: 180   Origin: Round 1, 2015 Draft (#3 overall)

YEAR	TEAM	LVL	AGE	PA	R	2B	3B	HR	RBI	BB	K	SB	CS	AVG/OBP/SLG
2017	LNC	A+	20	236	44	21	3	12	47	6	35	2	1	.387/.407/.671
2017	HFD	AA	20	164	20	5	0	6	17	8	36	0	2	.260/.323/.413
2018	HFD	AA	21	402	49	23	2	17	62	30	76	12	3	.275/.342/.493
2018	ABQ	AAA	21	72	5	4	0	0	5	1	16	0	0	.232/.264/.290
2019	ABQ	AAA	22	160	34	10	1	9	21	14	27	0	0	.350/.413/.622
2019	COL	MLB	22	81	8	2	0	0	7	4	27	0	0	.224/.272/.250
2020	COL	MLB	23	154	17	7	1	6	20	9	41	1	0	.258/.310/.436

Comparables: Jonathan Villar, Alen Hanson, Richard Ureña

After helping Celtic to become the first team in Scottish football history to win the treble in consecutive seasons, Rodgers departed for Leicester City in February, where he quickly … what? Baseball? Oh, you mean the *other* Brendan Rodgers. His 2019 didn't go as well as his namesake's across the pond. The Rockies infielder got his first shot at the big leagues but whiffed a ton and displayed almost no power. While a Colorado prospect's failing to make an impact in their first taste of the bigs is nothing new, the torn labrum that ended his season gives Rodgers another obstacle to a successful sophomore season on top of adjusting to the Show and finding time in a crowded infield. It probably won't be much consolation for him to learn that Leicester look terrific this season.

YEAR	TEAM	LVL	AGE	PA	DRC+	VORP	BABIP	BRR	FRAA	WARP
2017	LNC	A+	20	236	173	26.5	.413	0.9	SS(47): -5.6, 2B(4): -0.6	2.2
2017	HFD	AA	20	164	100	6.5	.306	-0.5	SS(33): -1.2, 2B(6): 0.3	0.5
2018	HFD	AA	21	402	112	27.4	.301	0.6	SS(58): -6.7, 2B(21): -2.1	1.5
2018	ABQ	AAA	21	72	52	-2.8	.302	-0.3	SS(11): -1.8, 3B(4): -0.2	-0.4
2019	ABQ	AAA	22	160	130	20.2	.380	2.0	2B(27): -1.9, SS(6): -0.1	1.2
2019	COL	MLB	22	81	47	-2.7	.347	1.5	2B(16): 1.1, SS(9): -1.1	-0.1
2020	COL	MLB	23	154	84	2.2	.323	-0.1	2B 0, SS -1	0.1

Brendan Rodgers, continued

Batted Ball Distribution

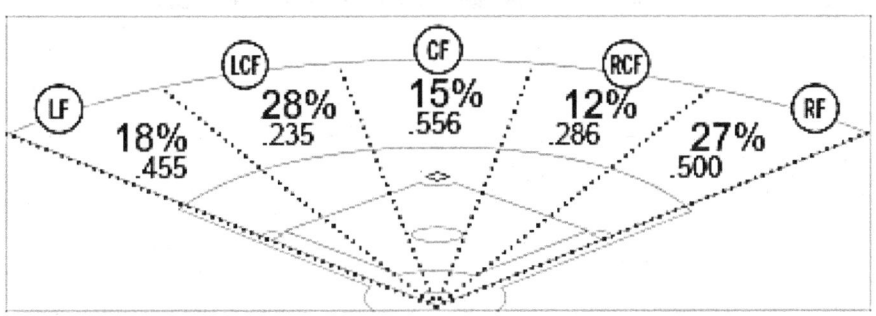

Strike Zone vs LHP   **Strike Zone vs RHP**

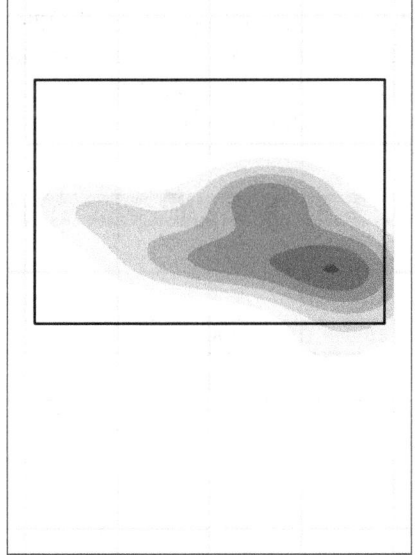

Trevor Story SS

Born: 11/15/92   Age: 27   Bats: R   Throws: R
Height: 6'2"   Weight: 214   Origin: Round 1, 2011 Draft (#45 overall)

YEAR	TEAM	LVL	AGE	PA	R	2B	3B	HR	RBI	BB	K	SB	CS	AVG/OBP/SLG
2017	COL	MLB	24	555	68	32	3	24	82	49	191	7	2	.239/.308/.457
2018	COL	MLB	25	656	88	42	6	37	108	47	168	27	6	.291/.348/.567
2019	COL	MLB	26	656	111	38	5	35	85	58	174	23	8	.294/.363/.554
2020	COL	MLB	27	595	82	32	6	32	95	52	165	16	5	.280/.349/.542

Comparables: Javier Báez, Jonathan Villar, Junior Lake

You've heard all the Story puns by now, so let's make it through this without one. His performance has been worthy of far more than a quip in any case. Story consolidated his success from 2018, demonstrating the kind of high-end consistency for his neighbor at third base has become known. That osmosis hasn't quite extended to the defensive side of the game, but Story's no joke with the glove either. He was a worthy All-Star for the second season running, and while he's a tier below the true MVP candidates, he's knocking on the door to that club. Even though there are still plenty of strikeouts, the Rockies shortstop has made a mockery of the notion that the swing-and-miss issues in his game were too much to overcome. Two more years remain before Story hits the open market, as much as fans might wish his tenure was never-ending (almost made it).

YEAR	TEAM	LVL	AGE	PA	DRC+	VORP	BABIP	BRR	FRAA	WARP
2017	COL	MLB	24	555	92	27.6	.332	4.2	SS(142): -0.4	2.4
2018	COL	MLB	25	656	128	52.7	.345	-0.8	SS(156): -2.0	5.0
2019	COL	MLB	26	656	118	47.3	.361	3.5	SS(144): -0.3	4.9
2020	COL	MLB	27	595	115	35.9	.347	1.4	SS -2	3.5

Trevor Story, continued

Batted Ball Distribution

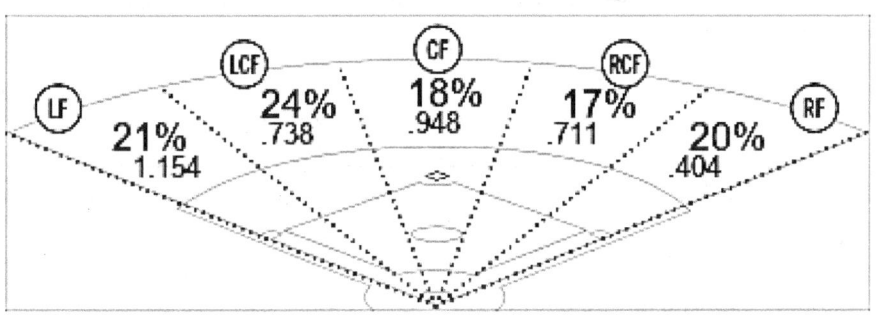

Strike Zone vs LHP   Strike Zone vs RHP

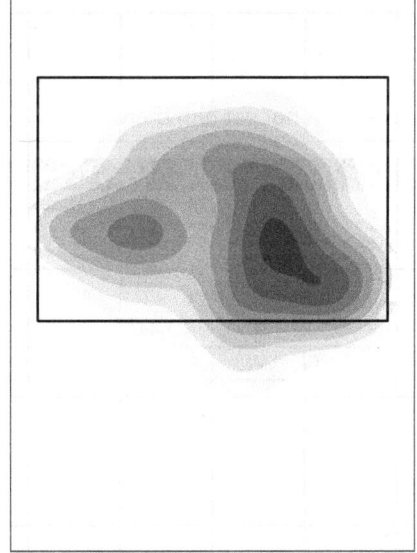

Raimel Tapia LF

Born: 02/04/94   Age: 26   Bats: L   Throws: L
Height: 6'3"   Weight: 185   Origin: International Free Agent, 2010

YEAR	TEAM	LVL	AGE	PA	R	2B	3B	HR	RBI	BB	K	SB	CS	AVG/OBP/SLG
2017	ABQ	AAA	23	277	45	20	8	2	30	13	42	12	2	.369/.397/.529
2017	COL	MLB	23	171	27	12	2	2	16	8	36	5	2	.288/.329/.425
2018	ABQ	AAA	24	473	81	33	9	11	62	32	85	21	3	.302/.352/.495
2018	COL	MLB	24	27	6	2	1	1	6	2	7	0	0	.200/.259/.480
2019	COL	MLB	25	447	54	23	5	9	44	21	100	9	3	.275/.309/.415
2020	COL	MLB	26	413	40	20	5	8	43	21	95	12	5	.266/.307/.403

Comparables: Victor Reyes, Brandon Drury, Sócrates Brito

Naturally, Tapia hit for average in 2019, even if it wasn't the .300-plus he managed in the minors. With his options exhausted, he got to stick around on the major-league roster all season. The continued exposure didn't give Tapia the chance to show what he can do as much as demonstrate what he can't: hit for power. The ball simply doesn't come off the bat that hard, whether in the air or on the ground. Given that he also doesn't take a ton of walks or play a particularly impressive outfield, Tapia's chances of making it as an everyday player hinge even more on his ability to hit for average. In truth, even hitting .300 might not get him there if he can't squeeze out more production elsewhere.

YEAR	TEAM	LVL	AGE	PA	DRC+	VORP	BABIP	BRR	FRAA	WARP
2017	ABQ	AAA	23	277	121	20.0	.432	-0.1	CF(48): 0.0, LF(5): -0.6	1.5
2017	COL	MLB	23	171	80	3.7	.361	1.6	RF(22): -3.0, LF(18): -1.3	-0.3
2018	ABQ	AAA	24	473	99	16.1	.354	1.4	CF(65): -5.2, RF(24): 0.0	0.8
2018	COL	MLB	24	27	87	0.7	.235	0.7	CF(6): -0.4, LF(1): 0.0	0.1
2019	COL	MLB	25	447	80	0.9	.341	-0.4	LF(91): 1.7, CF(13): -0.4	0.1
2020	COL	MLB	26	413	79	0.9	.334	0.6	LF -2, CF 0	-0.1

Raimel Tapia, continued

Batted Ball Distribution

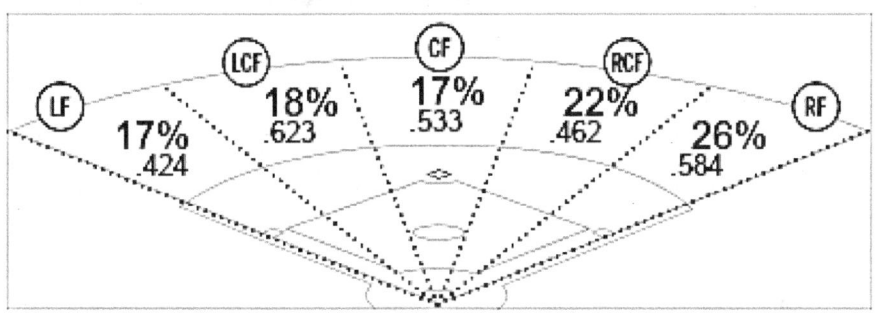

Strike Zone vs LHP   **Strike Zone vs RHP**

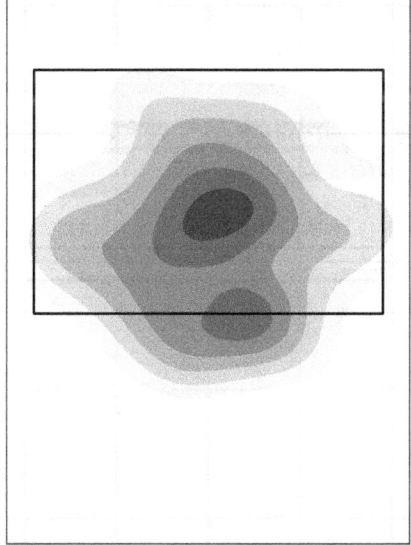

Colorado Rockies 2020

Colton Welker 3B

Born: 10/09/97 Age: 22 Bats: R Throws: R
Height: 6'1" Weight: 195 Origin: Round 4, 2016 Draft (#110 overall)

YEAR	TEAM	LVL	AGE	PA	R	2B	3B	HR	RBI	BB	K	SB	CS	AVG/OBP/SLG
2017	ASH	A	19	279	32	18	1	6	33	18	42	5	7	.350/.401/.500
2018	LNC	A+	20	509	74	32	0	13	82	42	103	5	1	.333/.383/.489
2019	HFD	AA	21	394	37	23	1	10	53	32	68	2	1	.252/.313/.408
2020	COL	MLB	22	251	24	13	0	6	27	16	57	1	0	.245/.296/.384

Comparables: Renato Núñez, Nolan Arenado, Gabriel Guerrero

Welker started out hot at Double-A and looked as though he would breeze through the level like every other assignment he's had. Then, he ran into his first signs of adversity. A lifeless June dropped his batting average well below .300 for the first time as a pro, and he was on the injured list by mid-July with a left shoulder impingement. That cost him a month, and Welker headed to the Arizona Fall League to make up for lost time, where he continued to struggle. If Welker can adjust against higher-level pitching, the bat speed and concurrent raw power will be thrilling to see in game action. For the first time in affiliated ball, however, he has thrown up questions about whether he'll be able to take that final step.

YEAR	TEAM	LVL	AGE	PA	DRC+	VORP	BABIP	BRR	FRAA	WARP
2017	ASH	A	19	279	156	19.4	.399	-1.6	3B(52): -7.3	1.5
2018	LNC	A+	20	509	138	30.1	.395	1.1	3B(92): -9.3, 1B(6): -0.7	2.6
2019	HFD	AA	21	394	113	6.9	.281	-2.8	3B(63): -1.5, 1B(27): 2.2	1.3
2020	COL	MLB	22	251	79	0.6	.298	-0.5	3B -4, 1B 0	-0.4

Colton Welker, continued

Batted Ball Distribution

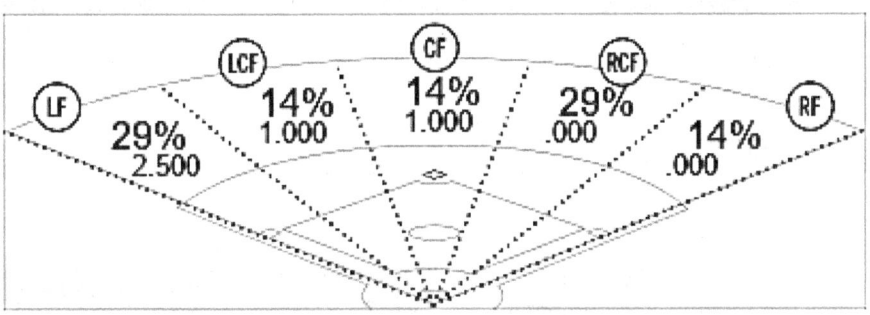

Strike Zone vs LHP **Strike Zone vs RHP**

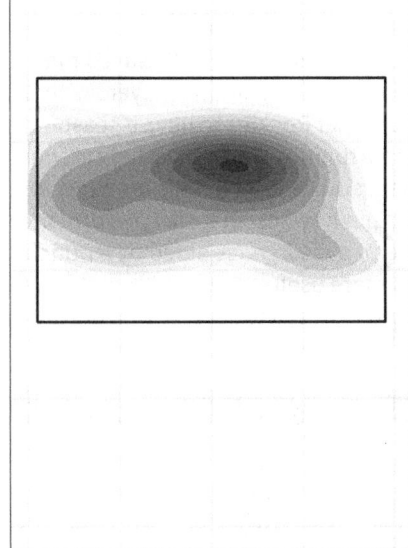

Tony Wolters C

Born: 06/09/92 Age: 28 Bats: L Throws: R
Height: 5'10" Weight: 197 Origin: Round 3, 2010 Draft (#87 overall)

YEAR	TEAM	LVL	AGE	PA	R	2B	3B	HR	RBI	BB	K	SB	CS	AVG/OBP/SLG
2017	ABQ	AAA	25	58	6	5	1	2	9	3	15	0	1	.259/.310/.500
2017	COL	MLB	25	266	30	8	1	0	16	33	55	0	1	.240/.341/.284
2018	COL	MLB	26	216	19	4	4	3	27	26	33	2	0	.170/.292/.286
2019	COL	MLB	27	411	42	17	2	1	42	36	68	0	1	.262/.337/.329
2020	COL	MLB	28	427	39	20	3	5	38	39	80	3	2	.246/.326/.351

Comparables: Tucker Barnhart, Smoky Burgess, Omar Narváez

Wolters stood out in 2019. In the most home run-friendly environment in major-league history—in terms of both park and league—he managed just one in over 400 trips to the plate. That was dead last among players with that many plate appearances and only Billy Hamilton (zero in 353 PA) saved him from being last among players with 300-plus. Wolters also joined a group of just four other Rockies to have a season with just a single homer in at least 300 opportunities. The converted catcher has never had power, of course, with a mere six homers over his previous three seasons in Colorado. That helps to explain how his offensive performance actually improved, with his batting average resurgence aided by a bunch of ground balls traded for line drives. With his more useful stand-out tool (his framing) going in the wrong direction, Wolters needs to reverse that decline to be anything more than the wrong end of a Rockies fun fact.

YEAR	TEAM	P. COUNT	FRM RUNS	BLK RUNS	THRW RUNS	TOT RUNS
2017	ABQ	1747	2.3	0.0	0.1	2.6
2017	COL	9693	-2.7	-0.6	1.1	-3.0
2018	COL	7924	10.2	-0.6	0.2	9.6
2019	COL	15038	-8.8	1.4	1.1	-6.4
2020	COL	19233	6.9	0.3	1.6	8.8

YEAR	TEAM	LVL	AGE	PA	DRC+	VORP	BABIP	BRR	FRAA	WARP
2017	ABQ	AAA	25	58	90	3.8	.324	0.3	C(13): 1.9	0.4
2017	COL	MLB	25	266	75	0.6	.316	0.5	C(77): -0.9, 2B(4): 0.1	0.4
2018	COL	MLB	26	216	76	1.1	.189	2.5	C(64): 10.7, LF(2): 0.0	1.8
2019	COL	MLB	27	411	85	13.2	.314	3.4	C(112): -4.5, 2B(8): 0.0	1.2
2020	COL	MLB	28	427	78	10.0	.299	2.4	C 10	2.0

Tony Wolters, continued

Batted Ball Distribution

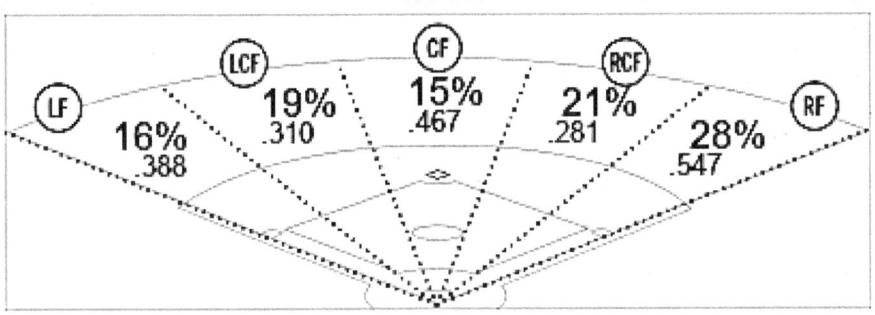

| Strike Zone vs LHP | Strike Zone vs RHP |

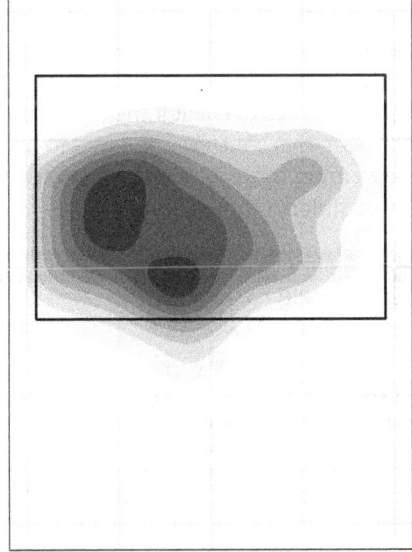

Colorado Rockies 2020

Yency Almonte   RHP
Born: 06/04/94   Age: 26   Bats: B   Throws: R
Height: 6'5"   Weight: 217   Origin: Round 17, 2012 Draft (#537 overall)

YEAR	TEAM	LVL	AGE	W	L	SV	G	GS	IP	H	HR	BB/9	K/9	K	GB%	BABIP
2017	HFD	AA	23	5	3	0	14	14	76^1	58	4	3.7	8.4	71	45%	.267
2017	ABQ	AAA	23	3	1	0	8	7	35	41	7	5.4	5.7	22	50%	.321
2018	ABQ	AAA	24	3	5	1	18	10	43^2	44	8	2.9	7.0	34	45%	.283
2018	COL	MLB	24	0	0	0	14	0	14^2	15	1	2.5	8.6	14	48%	.341
2019	ABQ	AAA	25	2	3	5	30	0	30	29	2	7.8	9.6	32	49%	.318
2019	COL	MLB	25	0	1	0	28	0	34	39	7	3.7	7.7	29	34%	.302
2020	COL	MLB	26	2	2	0	33	0	35	38	6	4.3	8.5	33	40%	.317

Comparables: Chase De Jong, Hunter Wood, Brad Peacock

Like many of his colleagues, Almonte suffered some serious regression after a promising 2018. While the fastball still touches 98, that helps very little when it is frequently returned with significant interest. The 25-year-old simply stopped missing bats with the heater as the season went on and finished the year with opponents slugging .781 against the pitch. The slider is still a real weapon: Almonte now has 39 strikeouts to just one walk with the pitch since his debut, with a .146 batting average allowed. The question is whether he will get enough opportunities to use it if the four-seam remains this ineffective. By the end of the year, this contrast appeared to have some material effects on his usage, as September represented the first month of his career in which Almonte threw more sliders than fastballs.

YEAR	TEAM	LVL	AGE	WHIP	ERA	DRA	WARP	MPH	FB%	WHF	CSP
2017	HFD	AA	23	1.17	2.00	3.19	1.8				
2017	ABQ	AAA	23	1.77	4.89	6.92	-0.5				
2018	ABQ	AAA	24	1.33	5.56	4.44	0.5				
2018	COL	MLB	24	1.30	1.84	4.37	0.1	97.3	63	13.5	45.8
2019	ABQ	AAA	25	1.83	4.20	4.88	0.4				
2019	COL	MLB	25	1.56	5.56	6.39	-0.4	97.4	56.8	12.1	45.2
2020	COL	MLB	26	1.57	5.67	5.07	0.1	97.0	59.4	12.7	46.3

Yency Almonte, continued

Pitch Shape vs LHH

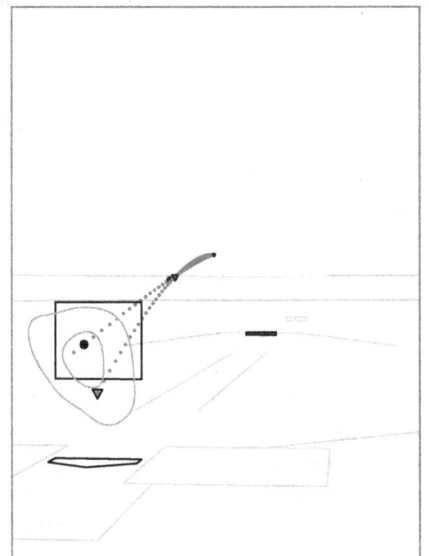

Pitch Shape vs RHH

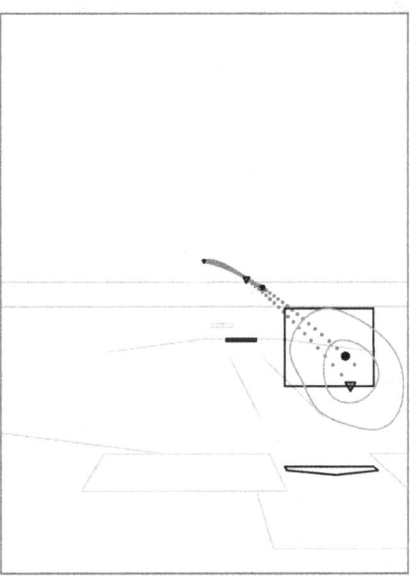

Type	Frequency	Velocity	H Movement	V Movement
● Fastball	56.8%	95.8 [110]	-7.6 [97]	-14.7 [103]
☐ Sinker				
+ Cutter				
▲ Changeup				
✕ Splitter				
▽ Slider	40.2%	85.9 [106]	4.8 [99]	-32.3 [102]
◇ Curveball				
✦ Slow Curveball				
✳ Knuckleball				
▼ Screwball				

Wade Davis RHP

Born: 09/07/85 Age: 34 Bats: R Throws: R
Height: 6'5" Weight: 227 Origin: Round 3, 2004 Draft (#75 overall)

YEAR	TEAM	LVL	AGE	W	L	SV	G	GS	IP	H	HR	BB/9	K/9	K	GB%	BABIP
2017	CHN	MLB	31	4	2	32	59	0	58^2	39	6	4.3	12.1	79	42%	.262
2018	COL	MLB	32	3	6	43	69	0	65^1	43	8	3.6	10.7	78	42%	.238
2019	COL	MLB	33	1	6	15	50	0	42^2	51	7	6.1	8.9	42	40%	.349
2020	COL	MLB	34	3	2	9	50	0	52	49	8	4.5	9.9	58	41%	.301

Comparables: Jason Isringhausen, Daniel Hudson, Jim Gott

The warning signs have been there for Davis since his year in Chicago, when his velocity was starting to dip and he began nibbling around the zone to compensate. Now the demoted closer isn't throwing any harder than when he was a starter, and the results were much, much worse. No longer able to challenge hitters in the zone with his fastball at all, Davis has seen his secondary pitches lose effectiveness too. The loss in velocity hasn't helped his walk rate either. A violent reversal of his BABIP fortune from 2018 completed this run-per-inning recipe for disaster. A move to the bullpen once rejuvenated Davis, but there's no transition the 34-year-old could make that would have remotely the same effect. At this point, the Rockies will have to hope for respectable middle reliever and brace themselves for worse.

YEAR	TEAM	LVL	AGE	WHIP	ERA	DRA	WARP	MPH	FB%	WHF	CSP
2017	CHN	MLB	31	1.14	2.30	2.78	1.6	96.4	47.6	16	41.8
2018	COL	MLB	32	1.06	4.13	3.90	0.8	95.9	49	12.7	40.1
2019	COL	MLB	33	1.88	8.65	6.31	-0.4	95.0	46.3	11.1	41
2020	COL	MLB	34	1.43	4.53	4.16	0.7	94.6	46.9	12.8	40.3

Wade Davis, continued

Pitch Shape vs LHH

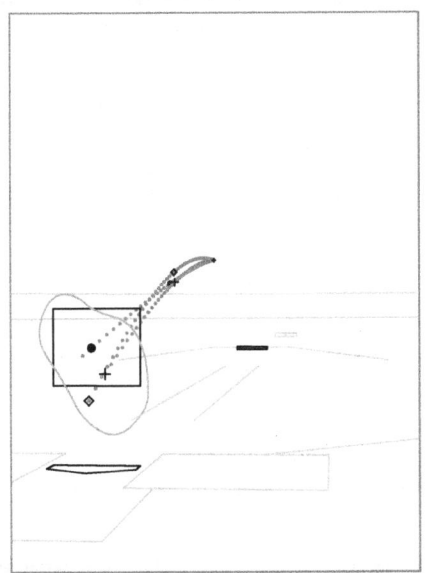

Pitch Shape vs RHH

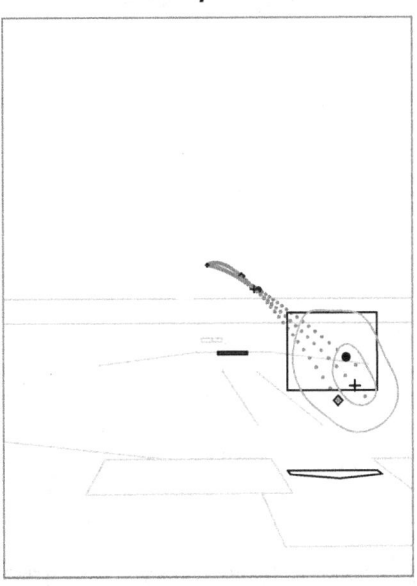

Type	Frequency	Velocity	H Movement	V Movement
● Fastball	44.7%	93.3 [103]	-1.8 [122]	-13.6 [106]
□ Sinker				
+ Cutter	34.8%	89 [102]	4.3 [115]	-25.2 [96]
▲ Changeup				
✕ Splitter				
▽ Slider				
◇ Curveball	19.0%	82.9 [114]	5.7 [93]	-43.8 [108]
⊕ Slow Curveball				
✳ Knuckleball				
▼ Screwball				

Phillip Diehl LHP

Born: 07/16/94 Age: 25 Bats: L Throws: L
Height: 6'2" Weight: 180 Origin: Round 27, 2016 Draft (#818 overall)

YEAR	TEAM	LVL	AGE	W	L	SV	G	GS	IP	H	HR	BB/9	K/9	K	GB%	BABIP
2017	CSC	A	22	9	3	2	28	5	85^1	76	4	2.7	10.7	101	49%	.329
2018	TAM	A+	23	2	2	3	25	0	48^2	37	2	2.2	14.6	79	43%	.357
2018	TRN	AA	23	0	1	1	14	0	26^2	18	2	3.7	9.8	29	35%	.254
2019	HFD	AA	24	0	0	0	11	0	13^1	5	0	2.0	8.1	12	58%	.161
2019	ABQ	AAA	24	2	1	0	39	0	45^1	54	16	3.0	10.3	52	37%	.333
2019	COL	MLB	24	0	0	0	10	0	7^1	10	1	2.5	9.8	8	21%	.391
2020	COL	MLB	25	1	1	0	22	0	23	24	5	3.7	10.7	28	35%	.317

Comparables: James Pazos, Steven Matz, Kevin Chapman

Traded to Colorado last offseason for Mike Tauchman, Diehl cruised through his assignment to Double-A Hartford without giving up a single run to earn a promotion to Albuquerque. Meanwhile, Tauchman had a .641 OPS in his first month filling in for the injury-riddled Yankees. Diehl and his low-90s fastball didn't take so well to pitching at altitude: he allowed 41 runs in his next 49 appearances across Triple-A and the majors. As for Tauchman's season...let's just say it went in the opposite direction.

YEAR	TEAM	LVL	AGE	WHIP	ERA	DRA	WARP	MPH	FB%	WHF	CSP
2017	CSC	A	22	1.20	3.16	4.13	0.9				
2018	TAM	A+	23	1.01	3.14	2.57	1.3				
2018	TRN	AA	23	1.09	1.35	3.70	0.4				
2019	HFD	AA	24	0.60	0.00	2.88	0.3				
2019	ABQ	AAA	24	1.52	6.75	6.17	0.0				
2019	COL	MLB	24	1.64	7.36	6.25	-0.1	91.8	44.9	18.1	41.8
2020	COL	MLB	25	1.43	5.19	4.77	0.2	91.5	46	18.6	42.8

Phillip Diehl, continued

Pitch Shape vs LHH

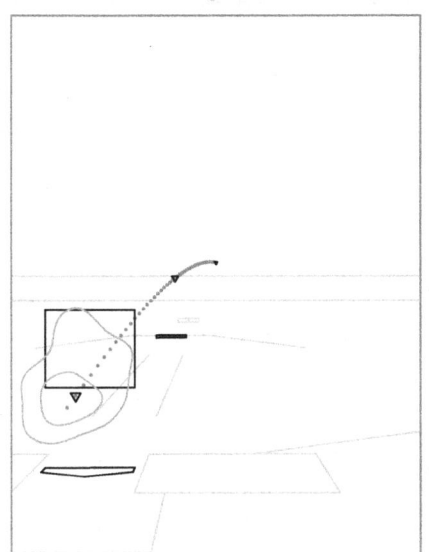

Pitch Shape vs RHH

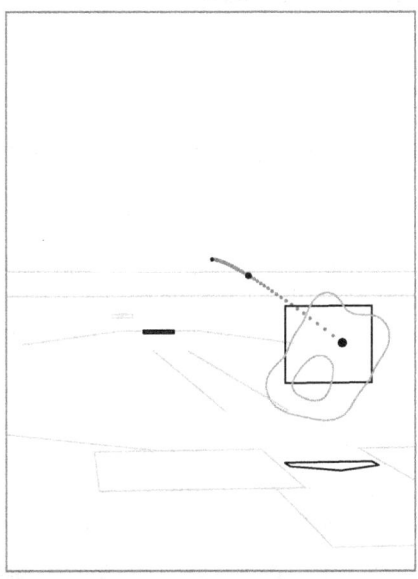

Type	Frequency	Velocity	H Movement	V Movement
● Fastball	44.9%	90.9 [96]	10.4 [84]	-17.4 [96]
☐ Sinker				
+ Cutter				
▲ Changeup				
✕ Splitter				
▽ Slider	55.1%	81.1 [86]	-1.2 [84]	-39.2 [82]
◇ Curveball				
⊕ Slow Curveball				
✳ Knuckleball				
▼ Screwball				

Jairo Díaz RHP

Born: 05/27/91   Age: 29   Bats: R   Throws: R
Height: 6'0"   Weight: 200   Origin: International Free Agent, 2007

YEAR	TEAM	LVL	AGE	W	L	SV	G	GS	IP	H	HR	BB/9	K/9	K	GB%	BABIP
2017	ABQ	AAA	26	0	1	3	20	0	18	16	1	3.5	8.5	17	56%	.306
2017	COL	MLB	26	0	0	0	4	0	5	12	0	9.0	3.6	2	59%	.545
2019	ABQ	AAA	28	1	0	6	16	0	20	12	0	2.7	9.9	22	65%	.250
2019	COL	MLB	28	6	4	5	56	0	57^2	56	7	3.0	9.8	63	50%	.318
2020	COL	MLB	29	3	3	3	55	0	58	61	8	3.7	10.3	67	52%	.340

Comparables: Jose A. Valdez, Hansel Robles, Kevin Jepsen

After a long and complicated road back from Tommy John surgery, Díaz emphatically turned the corner to open 2019 with just a single earned run given up over 20 Triple-A innings. That earned him the call back to the majors in mid-May, and he would stick around for the rest of the year. With his fastball touching 99, wipeout slider in full effect, and control finally harnessed, Díaz earned the trust of Bud Black and became the closer in September. A few bad outings inflated his ERA, but his overall park-adjusted performance was well above-average. Whether he gets another shot at closing likely depends on Wade Davis and Scott Oberg more than Díaz himself, but he's clearly next in line.

YEAR	TEAM	LVL	AGE	WHIP	ERA	DRA	WARP	MPH	FB%	WHF	CSP
2017	ABQ	AAA	26	1.28	5.00	3.18	0.4				
2017	COL	MLB	26	3.40	9.00	7.96	-0.2	100.1	77.3	5	43.2
2019	ABQ	AAA	28	0.90	0.45	1.54	0.9				
2019	COL	MLB	28	1.30	4.53	3.49	1.2	98.8	56	15.2	47.7
2020	COL	MLB	29	1.47	4.77	4.33	0.7	98.2	57.6	14.5	46

Jairo Díaz, continued

Pitch Shape vs LHH

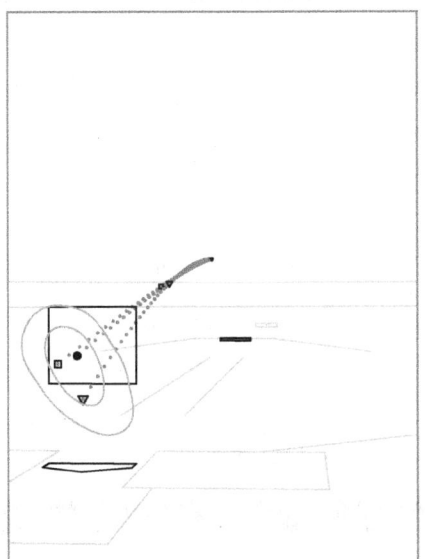

Pitch Shape vs RHH

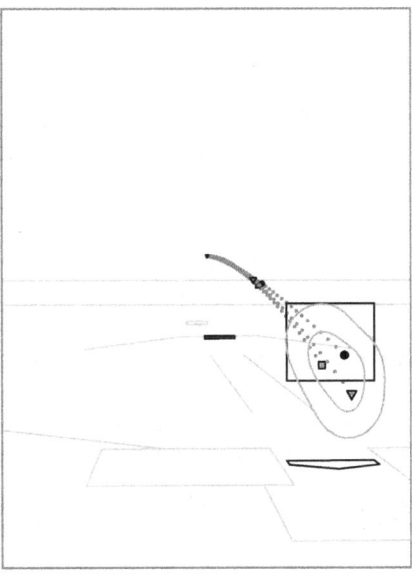

Type	Frequency	Velocity	H Movement	V Movement
● Fastball	30.6%	97.2 [114]	-4.8 [109]	-13.8 [106]
□ Sinker	25.5%	96.7 [121]	-11.3 [109]	-17.7 [109]
+ Cutter				
▲ Changeup				
✕ Splitter				
▽ Slider	44.0%	88.1 [116]	1.4 [85]	-31.6 [104]
◇ Curveball				
⊕ Slow Curveball				
✳ Knuckleball				
▼ Screwball				

Carlos Estévez RHP

Born: 12/28/92 Age: 27 Bats: R Throws: R
Height: 6'6" Weight: 275 Origin: International Free Agent, 2011

YEAR	TEAM	LVL	AGE	W	L	SV	G	GS	IP	H	HR	BB/9	K/9	K	GB%	BABIP
2017	ABQ	AAA	24	1	4	4	33	0	33²	23	2	2.7	9.1	34	60%	.253
2017	COL	MLB	24	5	0	0	35	0	32¹	39	3	3.9	8.6	31	47%	.360
2018	ABQ	AAA	25	0	1	1	28	0	28¹	37	6	3.5	11.1	35	39%	.397
2019	COL	MLB	26	2	2	0	71	0	72	70	12	2.9	10.1	81	39%	.304
2020	COL	MLB	27	3	3	0	55	0	58	57	9	3.3	10.5	68	40%	.319

Comparables: Jake Barrett, Michael Tonkin, John Gant

Estévez rebounded from a lost season in style by leading the team in appearances and relief innings to go along with a distinctly un-Coors ERA. A drop in his release point and increased reliance on his slider led to more strikeouts, fewer walks and a DRA 15 percent better than league-average. A flawless September was ruined in his very last appearance of the year as an Evan Longoria homer represented the only run he gave up all month. By that point, his case for a higher-leverage role was already well-made.

YEAR	TEAM	LVL	AGE	WHIP	ERA	DRA	WARP	MPH	FB%	WHF	CSP
2017	ABQ	AAA	24	0.98	1.34	1.93	1.2				
2017	COL	MLB	24	1.64	5.57	5.06	0.0	99.2	74.5	11.7	50
2018	ABQ	AAA	25	1.69	6.35	5.00	0.0				
2019	COL	MLB	26	1.29	3.75	4.09	1.0	99.6	69.3	15.1	52.7
2020	COL	MLB	27	1.34	4.29	3.97	0.9	99.0	71.3	14.5	52.3

Carlos Estévez, continued

Pitch Shape vs LHH	Pitch Shape vs RHH
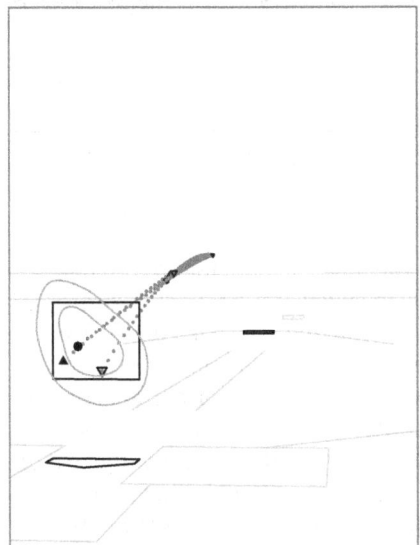	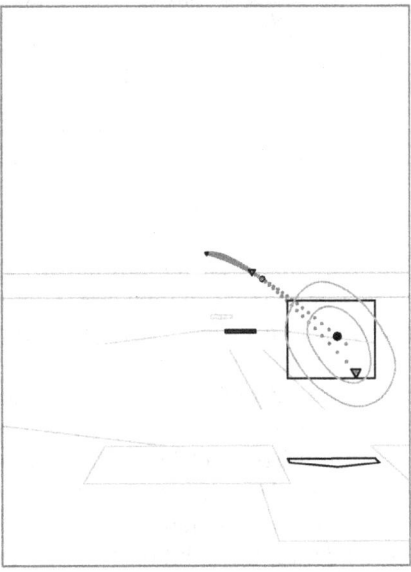

Type	Frequency	Velocity	H Movement	V Movement
● Fastball	69.0%	98 [116]	-5.3 [107]	-11.6 [111]
☐ Sinker				
+ Cutter				
▲ Changeup	3.5%	90.6 [119]	-10.2 [105]	-23.1 [113]
✕ Splitter				
▽ Slider	27.2%	87.8 [114]	5.3 [101]	-30.6 [107]
◇ Curveball				
✦ Slow Curveball				
✱ Knuckleball				
▼ Screwball				

Kyle Freeland LHP

Born: 05/14/93 Age: 27 Bats: L Throws: L
Height: 6'4" Weight: 201 Origin: Round 1, 2014 Draft (#8 overall)

YEAR	TEAM	LVL	AGE	W	L	SV	G	GS	IP	H	HR	BB/9	K/9	K	GB%	BABIP
2017	COL	MLB	24	11	11	0	33	28	156	169	17	3.6	6.2	107	56%	.308
2018	COL	MLB	25	17	7	0	33	33	202^1	182	17	3.1	7.7	173	48%	.285
2019	ABQ	AAA	26	0	4	0	6	6	29^2	40	4	4.9	8.5	28	60%	.379
2019	COL	MLB	26	3	11	0	22	22	104^1	126	25	3.4	6.8	79	48%	.308
2020	COL	MLB	27	7	9	0	24	24	122	140	19	3.5	7.3	98	49%	.322

Comparables: Brian Flynn, Ricky Romero, Wade LeBlanc

Buffy the Vampire Slayer introduced us to the term Big Bad, the overarching villain that the season-long plot ultimately revolved around. For Rockies pitchers, Coors Field is the Big Bad, and Freeland defeated it in 2018. In true supervillain fashion, Coors refused to simply roll over and quit, and instead plotted monstrous revenge. The memory of the best ERA by a starter in Coors history quickly faded as the new season started and dinger after dinger soared over the outfield wall. By the time he was demoted to the minors at the end of May, Freeland was just one round-tripper shy of tying his 17 homers allowed in 2018, a total accumulated over more than 200 innings. Essentially everything Freeland throws was hit harder, with the cutter, so effective last season, responsible for 10 homers alone, while the changeup lost separation in terms of both velocity and movement. A slightly reduced homer rate upon his return did little to improve the overall results. By the end of the year, his Coors ERA stood at 9.25, almost seven runs higher than it was in 2018. Buffy always eventually defeated the Big Bad for good. There's no real way to slay Coors Field—at least as long as the Rockies remain in Denver.

YEAR	TEAM	LVL	AGE	WHIP	ERA	DRA	WARP	MPH	FB%	WHF	CSP
2017	COL	MLB	24	1.49	4.10	5.91	-0.6	94.1	64.5	8.2	46.1
2018	COL	MLB	25	1.25	2.85	3.89	3.3	94.1	52.5	9.9	47.9
2019	ABQ	AAA	26	1.89	8.80	6.44	0.1				
2019	COL	MLB	26	1.58	6.73	6.30	-0.6	93.8	52.1	10.3	47
2020	COL	MLB	27	1.54	5.40	4.86	1.3	93.5	56.2	9.7	47.7

Kyle Freeland, continued

Pitch Shape vs LHH
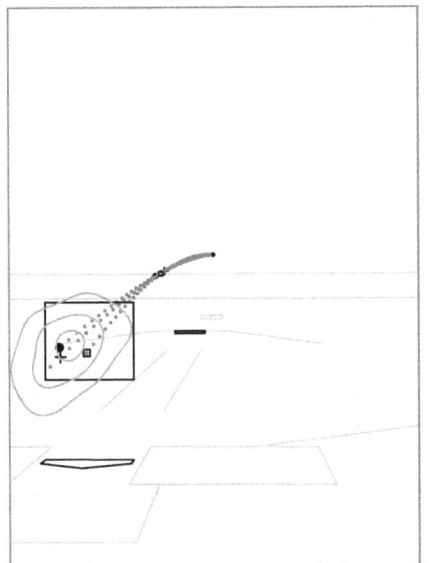

Pitch Shape vs RHH
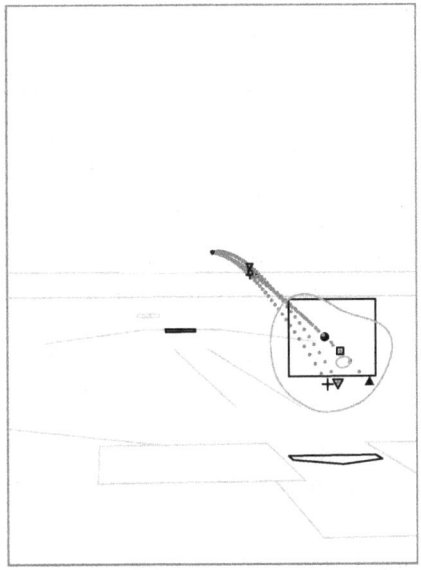

Type	Frequency	Velocity	H Movement	V Movement
● Fastball	41.5%	92.2 [99]	5.7 [105]	-16.4 [99]
☐ Sinker	10.6%	91.4 [94]	12.5 [101]	-23 [91]
+ Cutter	31.3%	86.9 [89]	-2.3 [103]	-27 [89]
▲ Changeup	11.0%	86.7 [105]	9.2 [109]	-26 [104]
✕ Splitter				
▽ Slider	5.6%	81.3 [87]	-2 [87]	-36.1 [91]
◇ Curveball				
✦ Slow Curveball				
✱ Knuckleball				
▼ Screwball				

Chi Chi González RHP

Born: 01/15/92 Age: 28 Bats: R Throws: R
Height: 6'3" Weight: 215 Origin: Round 1, 2013 Draft (#23 overall)

YEAR	TEAM	LVL	AGE	W	L	SV	G	GS	IP	H	HR	BB/9	K/9	K	GB%	BABIP
2019	ABQ	AAA	27	4	5	0	16	15	87	105	15	3.7	7.9	76	52%	.342
2019	COL	MLB	27	2	6	0	14	12	63	59	11	4.7	6.6	46	45%	.257
2020	COL	MLB	28	7	8	0	23	23	113	126	18	3.9	6.6	83	47%	.304

Comparables: Drew VerHagen, Kyle Ryan, Allen Webster

Following many years of development, salmon must undergo a grueling, dangerous journey to reach their ultimate goal. They need to swim upstream against the current, in some cases for hundreds of miles, while evading both natural predators and fishermen, in order to reach their spawning grounds. Many of them die during the journey, and even those that make it usually pass away not long after arrival, sometimes before they're even able to reproduce. González's journey back from Tommy John surgery was also long, challenging, and culminated at much higher ground without much success. He did ultimately put together some promising starts in September with signs of a rejuvenated changeup, and, unlike the salmon, he gets to come back next season and have another go.

YEAR	TEAM	LVL	AGE	WHIP	ERA	DRA	WARP	MPH	FB%	WHF	CSP
2019	ABQ	AAA	27	1.62	6.10	4.82	1.6				
2019	COL	MLB	27	1.46	5.29	6.16	-0.3	93.9	54.9	8.9	46.6
2020	COL	MLB	28	1.54	5.37	4.84	1.3	93.3	55.2	9	46.9

Chi Chi González, continued

Pitch Shape vs LHH

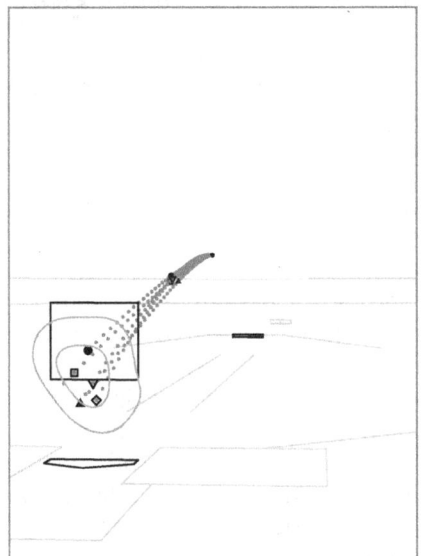

Pitch Shape vs RHH

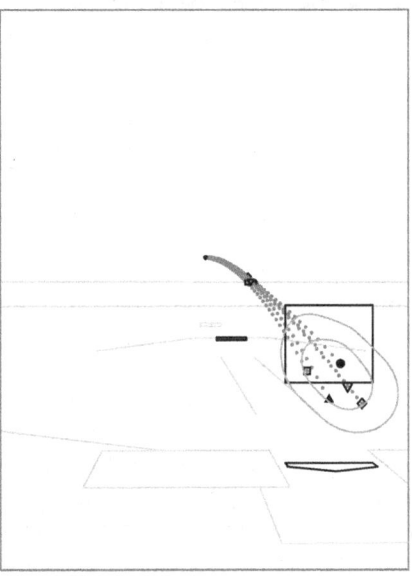

Type	Frequency	Velocity	H Movement	V Movement
● Fastball	42.5%	92.3 [100]	-2.9 [118]	-18.1 [94]
☐ Sinker	12.3%	91.4 [94]	-10.2 [116]	-22.5 [92]
+ Cutter				
▲ Changeup	11.0%	86.3 [104]	-10.6 [103]	-30.4 [91]
✕ Splitter				
▽ Slider	26.1%	87 [111]	2.1 [88]	-28 [115]
◇ Curveball	8.0%	82.5 [113]	4.3 [87]	-35.9 [125]
⬥ Slow Curveball				
✳ Knuckleball				
▼ Screwball				

Jon Gray RHP

Born: 11/05/91 Age: 28 Bats: R Throws: R
Height: 6'4" Weight: 227 Origin: Round 1, 2013 Draft (#3 overall)

YEAR	TEAM	LVL	AGE	W	L	SV	G	GS	IP	H	HR	BB/9	K/9	K	GB%	BABIP
2017	ABQ	AAA	25	0	0	0	2	2	9^1	10	2	4.8	12.5	13	48%	.348
2017	COL	MLB	25	10	4	0	20	20	110^1	113	10	2.4	9.1	112	49%	.336
2018	COL	MLB	26	12	9	0	31	31	172^1	180	27	2.7	9.6	183	49%	.323
2019	COL	MLB	27	11	8	0	26	25	150	147	19	3.4	9.0	150	52%	.314
2020	COL	MLB	28	9	9	0	26	26	156	163	21	3.4	9.7	167	50%	.330

Comparables: Vince Velasquez, Kevin Gausman, Dan Straily

Fifty might be too many shades even for a pitcher as inconsistent as Gray. Nonetheless, 2019 presented yet another version—or versions—of the starter who at various points in the last four years has looked like everything from the team's ace to back-of-the-rotation fodder with a cloudy future. By comparison to the rest of the rotation, this Gray was a bright spot, going deeper into games more consistently than ever before and simply keeping the team in them more often than anyone else. Yes, there were starts where he was simply off, and this wasn't the shining example of a rotation-leading workhorse we once hoped for. The hard contact alone also paints a dim picture of Gray's chance of ever truly reaching his ceiling. Still, while this season wasn't brilliant, it was still tinged with far more hope than the previous campaign.

YEAR	TEAM	LVL	AGE	WHIP	ERA	DRA	WARP	MPH	FB%	WHF	CSP
2017	ABQ	AAA	25	1.61	1.93	4.67	0.1				
2017	COL	MLB	25	1.30	3.67	3.32	2.8	98.0	57.4	9.9	49.8
2018	COL	MLB	26	1.35	5.12	4.45	1.7	97.4	49.7	13.3	48.7
2019	COL	MLB	27	1.35	3.84	3.97	2.9	98.0	52.7	12.4	48.6
2020	COL	MLB	28	1.43	4.64	4.24	2.7	97.2	52.7	12.3	49.2

Jon Gray, continued

Pitch Shape vs LHH

Pitch Shape vs RHH

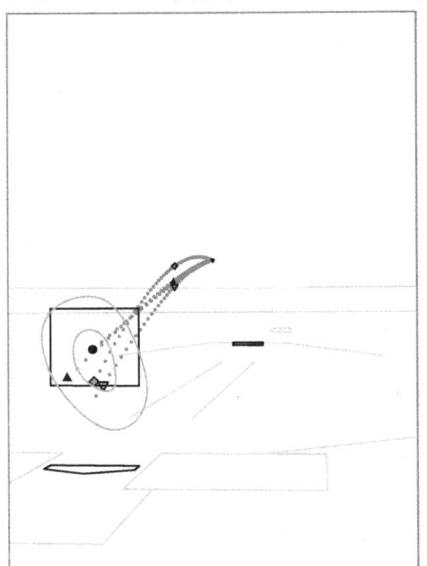
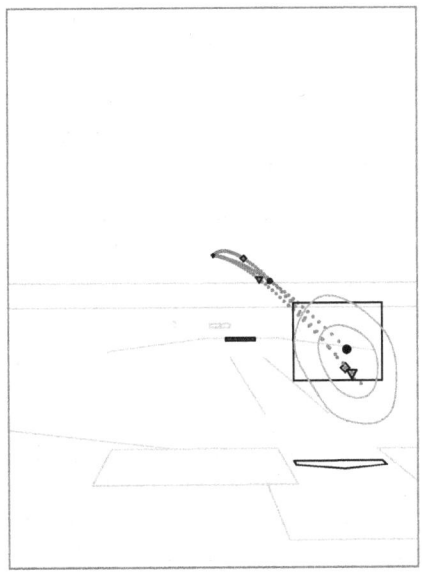

Type	Frequency	Velocity	H Movement	V Movement
● Fastball	52.3%	96.2 [111]	-9.6 [88]	-15.7 [101]
☐ Sinker				
+ Cutter				
▲ Changeup				
✕ Splitter				
▽ Slider	33.5%	88.5 [117]	1.6 [86]	-25.8 [121]
◇ Curveball	11.1%	78.8 [101]	9.2 [107]	-44.7 [106]
⊕ Slow Curveball				
✳ Knuckleball				
▼ Screwball				

Jeff Hoffman RHP

Born: 01/08/93 Age: 27 Bats: R Throws: R
Height: 6'5" Weight: 227 Origin: Round 1, 2014 Draft (#9 overall)

YEAR	TEAM	LVL	AGE	W	L	SV	G	GS	IP	H	HR	BB/9	K/9	K	GB%	BABIP
2017	ABQ	AAA	24	3	3	0	10	10	49²	44	3	3.4	8.5	47	46%	.285
2017	COL	MLB	24	6	5	0	23	16	99¹	106	15	3.6	7.4	82	42%	.304
2018	ABQ	AAA	25	6	8	0	21	21	105²	105	9	4.0	8.7	102	46%	.331
2018	COL	MLB	25	0	0	0	6	1	8²	15	0	7.3	5.2	5	53%	.469
2019	ABQ	AAA	26	6	8	0	17	16	85¹	105	19	3.2	10.3	98	44%	.361
2019	COL	MLB	26	2	6	0	15	15	70	77	21	4.4	8.7	68	37%	.298
2020	COL	MLB	27	6	8	0	32	21	113	128	22	3.8	8.0	101	41%	.316

Comparables: Aaron Blair, André Rienzo, Daniel Mengden

Hoffman spent three years as a consensus top-100 prospect, and it has been three years since his last appearance on such a list. That's long enough that the shine of that prospect pedigree has faded and been replaced by doubt—not just about whether Hoffman can ever live up to that pedigree, but about whether he can even cut it as a major leaguer. His four-seam fastball was one of the worst pitches in baseball, with Hoffman allowing extra-base hits more often than he struck hitters out. Every now and then, the stuff shows up and a hitter swings wildly over a curveball or fails to catch up to a heater that explodes past them. That only serves to make it more maddening when the command fails Hoffman so badly later in the game, if not that very same inning. At 27, with a 6.11 ERA in over 200 big-league innings, he's running out of chances to show he can start. A full-time move to the bullpen might both ameliorate his command issues and allow him to get back to pumping 99 with the fastball.

YEAR	TEAM	LVL	AGE	WHIP	ERA	DRA	WARP	MPH	FB%	WHF	CSP
2017	ABQ	AAA	24	1.27	4.71	2.51	1.7				
2017	COL	MLB	24	1.47	5.89	6.08	-0.6	97.0	67	8.9	50.7
2018	ABQ	AAA	25	1.44	4.94	4.24	1.6				
2018	COL	MLB	25	2.54	9.35	7.23	-0.2	95.0	53.9	8.9	42.8
2019	ABQ	AAA	26	1.58	7.70	5.54	1.0				
2019	COL	MLB	26	1.59	6.56	6.93	-0.9	95.7	58.8	10	47.8
2020	COL	MLB	27	1.56	5.85	5.23	0.7	95.8	62.6	9.6	47.4

Jeff Hoffman, continued

Pitch Shape vs LHH

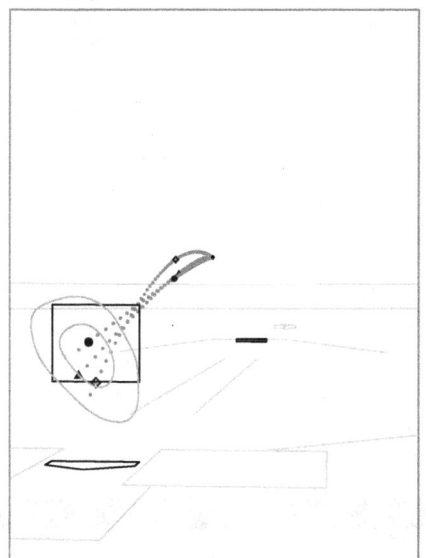

Pitch Shape vs RHH

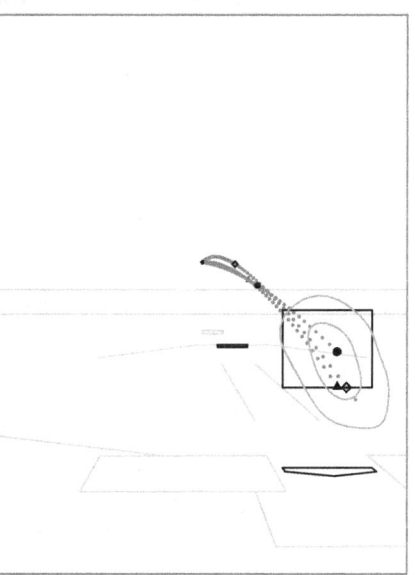

Type	Frequency	Velocity	H Movement	V Movement
● Fastball	58.8%	93.8 [104]	-10.3 [85]	-14.8 [103]
☐ Sinker				
+ Cutter				
▲ Changeup	11.4%	84.3 [97]	-9.6 [107]	-29.8 [93]
✕ Splitter				
▽ Slider				
◇ Curveball	28.8%	77.1 [95]	9.8 [110]	-52.1 [90]
⊕ Slow Curveball				
✱ Knuckleball				
▼ Screwball				

DJ Johnson RHP

Born: 08/30/89 Age: 30 Bats: L Throws: R
Height: 6'4" Weight: 230 Origin: Undrafted Free Agent, 2010

YEAR	TEAM	LVL	AGE	W	L	SV	G	GS	IP	H	HR	BB/9	K/9	K	GB%	BABIP
2017	HFD	AA	27	1	1	4	43	0	64^1	53	4	3.4	7.1	51	59%	.265
2018	ABQ	AAA	28	3	5	18	50	0	55^1	56	5	2.4	13.7	84	44%	.398
2018	COL	MLB	28	1	0	0	7	0	6^1	6	0	2.8	12.8	9	38%	.375
2019	ABQ	AAA	29	4	1	3	40	0	48	62	8	3.0	12.6	67	48%	.429
2019	COL	MLB	29	0	2	0	28	0	25	23	1	6.8	8.6	24	46%	.319
2020	COL	MLB	30	2	2	0	33	0	35	32	5	3.3	8.9	34	45%	.285

Comparables: Kevin Shackelford, Andrew Kittredge, Jacob Barnes

An appearance in the 2018 postseason after an epic journey to the majors proved to be the biggest splash Johnson made in a Rockies uniform. He added opening day roster to his list of firsts, but failed to get enough hitters to bite on his slider and ended up with far too many walks on his line. Before he got the hook from the Colorado roster, Johnson seized the opportunity to pitch elsewhere in late October, crossing the Pacific to join the Hiroshima Carp.

YEAR	TEAM	LVL	AGE	WHIP	ERA	DRA	WARP	MPH	FB%	WHF	CSP
2017	HFD	AA	27	1.20	2.80	3.33	1.1				
2018	ABQ	AAA	28	1.28	3.90	3.09	1.3				
2018	COL	MLB	28	1.26	4.26	4.70	0.0	95.4	44.8	16.2	44.8
2019	ABQ	AAA	29	1.62	5.62	4.78	0.7				
2019	COL	MLB	29	1.68	5.04	5.94	-0.2	94.9	58.3	11.9	48.2
2020	COL	MLB	30	1.28	3.83	4.07	0.5	94.2	56.1	12.5	46.5

DJ Johnson, continued

Pitch Shape vs LHH

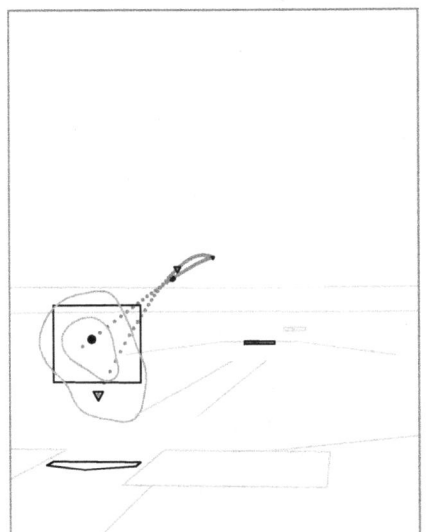

Pitch Shape vs RHH

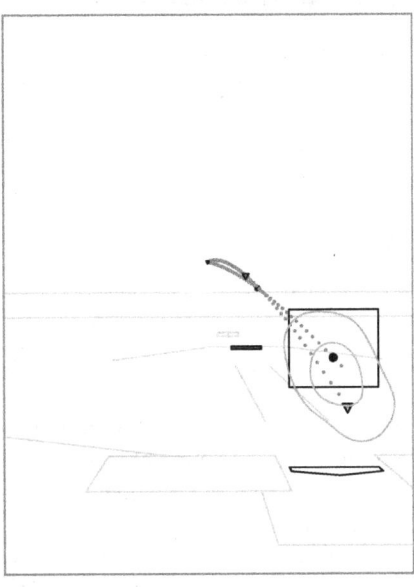

Type	Frequency	Velocity	H Movement	V Movement
● Fastball	58.3%	93.6 [103]	-5.8 [105]	-13.7 [106]
☐ Sinker				
+ Cutter	5.3%	91.4 [117]	-1.2 [82]	-20.4 [114]
▲ Changeup				
✕ Splitter				
▽ Slider	36.2%	82.6 [92]	4.3 [97]	-44.7 [66]
◇ Curveball				
⊕ Slow Curveball				
✱ Knuckleball				
▼ Screwball				

Peter Lambert RHP

Born: 04/18/97 Age: 23 Bats: R Throws: R
Height: 6'2" Weight: 185 Origin: Round 2, 2015 Draft (#44 overall)

YEAR	TEAM	LVL	AGE	W	L	SV	G	GS	IP	H	HR	BB/9	K/9	K	GB%	BABIP
2017	LNC	A+	20	9	8	0	26	26	142^1	147	18	1.9	8.3	131	43%	.321
2018	HFD	AA	21	8	2	0	15	15	92^2	80	6	1.2	7.3	75	50%	.282
2018	ABQ	AAA	21	2	5	0	11	11	55^1	72	5	2.4	5.0	31	52%	.345
2019	ABQ	AAA	22	2	2	0	11	11	60^1	63	10	2.4	7.6	51	53%	.294
2019	COL	MLB	22	3	7	0	19	19	89^1	119	18	3.6	5.7	57	48%	.333
2020	COL	MLB	23	5	6	0	37	15	90	115	16	3.2	5.7	57	48%	.324

Comparables: Jarrod Parker, Héctor Rondón, Eric Hurley

Deserved Run Average is designed to isolate a pitcher's contribution from other factors like defense (the Rockies were dead last in Park Adjusted Defensive Efficiency) and park (enough said). This can have the effect of suggesting that Rockies pitcher seasons aren't nearly as bad as their ERA indicates. It is therefore particularly disheartening that Lambert, who ranked dead last in ERA among all pitchers with at least 70 innings, in fact had a worse DRA. It's no coincidence that the rookie had the second-worst swinging strike rate and sixth-worst strikeout rate among that same group. Lambert's lack of bat-missing stuff might play elsewhere given his strong command profile. At Coors, all it meant was that he deserved every bit of that 7.25 ERA, and then some.

YEAR	TEAM	LVL	AGE	WHIP	ERA	DRA	WARP	MPH	FB%	WHF	CSP
2017	LNC	A+	20	1.24	4.17	4.10	1.9				
2018	HFD	AA	21	0.99	2.23	3.19	2.3				
2018	ABQ	AAA	21	1.57	5.04	5.67	-0.1				
2019	ABQ	AAA	22	1.31	5.07	3.19	2.1				
2019	COL	MLB	22	1.74	7.25	7.43	-1.6	94.3	53	7.5	47.2
2020	COL	MLB	23	1.62	6.13	5.40	0.3	94.2	54.9	7.7	48.9

Peter Lambert, continued

Pitch Shape vs LHH

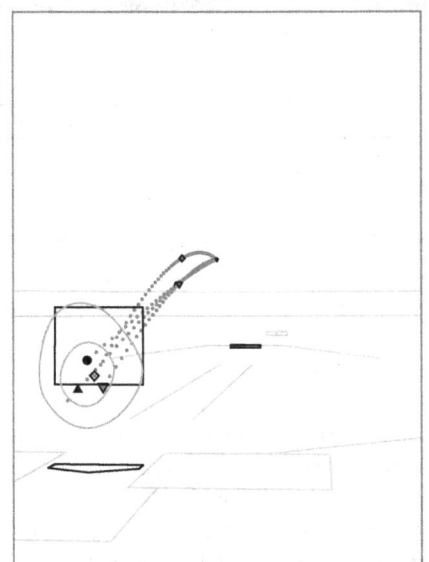

Pitch Shape vs RHH

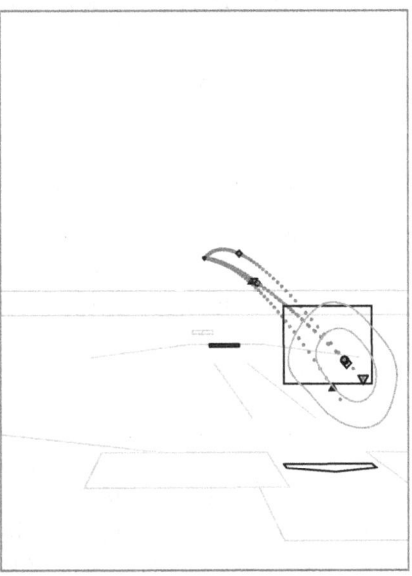

Type	Frequency	Velocity	H Movement	V Movement
● Fastball	53.0%	92.6 [101]	-7 [99]	-14.7 [103]
☐ Sinker				
+ Cutter				
▲ Changeup	21.5%	85.2 [100]	-8.5 [113]	-26.5 [103]
✕ Splitter				
▽ Slider	12.7%	87.5 [113]	2.6 [90]	-25.8 [121]
◇ Curveball	12.8%	77.9 [98]	4.8 [89]	-51.5 [92]
✦ Slow Curveball				
✳ Knuckleball				
▼ Screwball				

Jake McGee LHP

Born: 08/06/86 Age: 33 Bats: L Throws: L
Height: 6'4" Weight: 237 Origin: Round 5, 2004 Draft (#135 overall)

YEAR	TEAM	LVL	AGE	W	L	SV	G	GS	IP	H	HR	BB/9	K/9	K	GB%	BABIP
2017	COL	MLB	30	0	2	3	62	0	57¹	47	4	2.5	9.1	58	40%	.287
2018	COL	MLB	31	2	4	1	61	0	51¹	59	10	2.8	8.2	47	42%	.322
2019	COL	MLB	32	0	2	0	45	0	41¹	47	11	2.4	7.6	35	37%	.300
2020	COL	MLB	33	2	3	0	50	0	52	60	11	2.9	8.3	48	37%	.318

Comparables: Rafael Soriano, Jonathan Papelbon, Sean Doolittle

Rockies hurlers are used to their environment's making them look worse. In McGee's case, he had some company that made him seem better, as his ERA compared rather favorably to the other two expensive arms that were supposed to make up the back end of the Colorado bullpen. That's not to say that 2019 was a success, nor did it appear that the veteran southpaw deserved that number. The signs were encouraging early on, when McGee came out of the spring sitting 95 and touching 97 with his four-seamer. Then he sustained a knee sprain, never quite got the heat back when he returned, and suffered a second, more debilitating velocity drop mid-season that coincided with a truly brutal stretch over which hitters slugged .867 against the once-vaunted fastball. It was so bad that McGee actually started leaning on his second pitch, a hitherto unprecedented strategy. He either needs to incorporate the slider even more or figure out how to sustain the higher velo over a full season, because he simply can't compare to his former self without it.

YEAR	TEAM	LVL	AGE	WHIP	ERA	DRA	WARP	MPH	FB%	WHF	CSP
2017	COL	MLB	30	1.10	3.61	4.26	0.6	97.6	93.4	10.2	51.9
2018	COL	MLB	31	1.46	6.49	6.15	-0.7	96.6	86.3	11.1	53.2
2019	COL	MLB	32	1.40	4.35	6.33	-0.4	95.7	80.4	9.4	51.5
2020	COL	MLB	33	1.46	5.65	5.10	0.2	95.5	85.3	10.1	51.5

Jake McGee, continued

Pitch Shape vs LHH

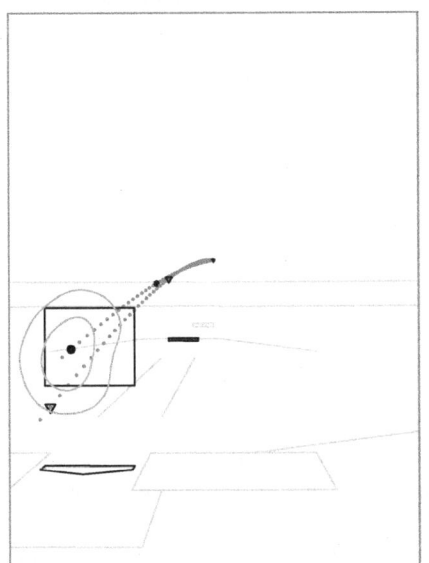

Pitch Shape vs RHH

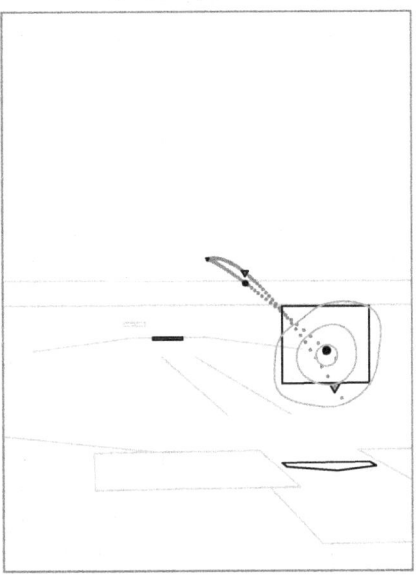

Type	Frequency	Velocity	H Movement	V Movement
● Fastball	80.4%	93.5 [103]	8.4 [93]	-14.8 [103]
☐ Sinker				
+ Cutter				
▲ Changeup				
✕ Splitter				
▽ Slider	19.2%	80.3 [83]	-2.2 [88]	-37.3 [88]
◇ Curveball				
✥ Slow Curveball				
✱ Knuckleball				
▼ Screwball				

Tim Melville   RHP

Born: 10/09/89   Age: 30   Bats: R   Throws: R
Height: 6'4"   Weight: 225   Origin: Round 4, 2008 Draft (#115 overall)

YEAR	TEAM	LVL	AGE	W	L	SV	G	GS	IP	H	HR	BB/9	K/9	K	GB%	BABIP
2017	ROC	AAA	27	4	3	0	11	10	66^2	48	5	3.1	8.6	64	36%	.246
2017	ELP	AAA	27	1	0	0	2	2	9^2	7	0	9.3	7.4	8	36%	.250
2017	MIN	MLB	27	0	1	0	1	1	3^1	4	1	8.1	10.8	4	50%	.333
2017	SDN	MLB	27	0	0	0	2	0	2^1	3	0	11.6	11.6	3	17%	.500
2018	NOR	AAA	28	9	6	4	40	14	104^2	115	15	3.6	7.1	82	39%	.311
2019	ABQ	AAA	29	10	5	0	18	17	96^1	113	24	3.7	8.8	94	42%	.320
2019	COL	MLB	29	2	3	0	7	7	33^1	34	9	3.8	6.5	24	45%	.263
2020	COL	MLB	30	2	2	0	33	0	35	37	7	4.0	7.4	29	40%	.285

Comparables: Matt Magill, Drew Gagnon, Josh A. Smith

Melville's indy-league-to-the-majors tale didn't turn out all that well in 2017 beyond the fact that he simply made the majors, so he rebooted the story in 2019. Once again, Melville went from the Long Island Ducks to Triple-A and, after a three-month wait, was back in the big leagues for his first truly successful major league start: seven innings of one-run ball against the Diamondbacks. He continued the fairytale by shutting out the Braves over five innings in his next start. That was as good as it got for the one-time top draft prospect. Given the frequency with which the entertainment industry recycles former projects, Melville might yet get another run at spinning this yarn into something even better than the first two versions.

YEAR	TEAM	LVL	AGE	WHIP	ERA	DRA	WARP	MPH	FB%	WHF	CSP
2017	ROC	AAA	27	1.07	2.70	2.86	2.1				
2017	ELP	AAA	27	1.76	4.66	5.35	0.0				
2017	MIN	MLB	27	2.10	13.50	6.36	0.0	96.0	59.8	8.5	36.6
2017	SDN	MLB	27	2.57	7.71	8.47	-0.1	96.3	67.3	7.7	42.7
2018	NOR	AAA	28	1.50	5.33	6.19	-0.9				
2019	ABQ	AAA	29	1.59	5.42	5.12	1.5				
2019	COL	MLB	29	1.44	4.86	6.21	-0.2	91.0	33.4	11.9	44.6
2020	COL	MLB	30	1.49	5.41	5.46	0.0	90.7	36.9	11.4	42.4

Tim Melville, continued

Pitch Shape vs LHH

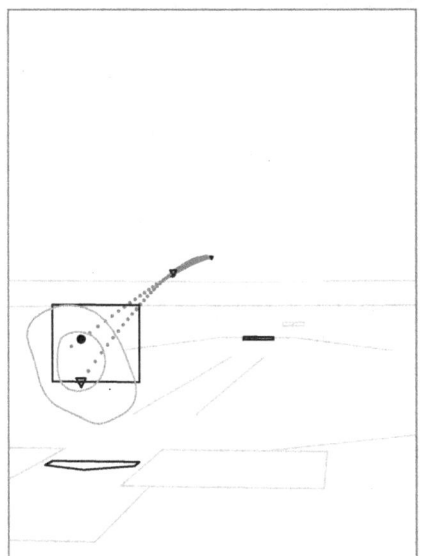

Pitch Shape vs RHH

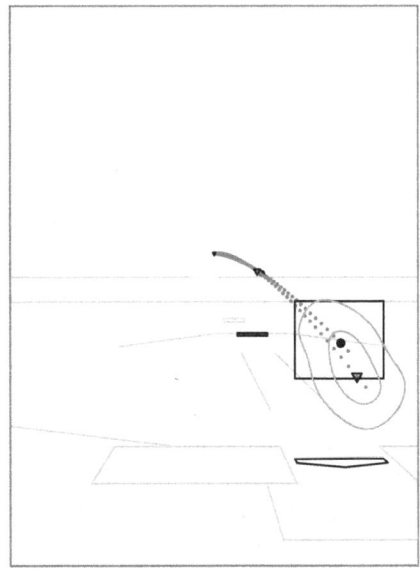

Type	Frequency	Velocity	H Movement	V Movement
● Fastball	33.4%	89.2 [91]	-7.7 [96]	-16.7 [98]
☐ Sinker				
+ Cutter				
▲ Changeup	6.6%	82.3 [89]	-11.7 [98]	-22.5 [114]
✕ Splitter				
▽ Slider	54.9%	83 [94]	1.5 [85]	-32.5 [102]
◇ Curveball	5.2%	75 [88]	3.2 [83]	-49.3 [96]
✦ Slow Curveball				
✱ Knuckleball				
▼ Screwball				

Colorado Rockies 2020

German Márquez   RHP
Born: 02/22/95 Age: 25 Bats: R Throws: R
Height: 6'1" Weight: 225 Origin: International Free Agent, 2011

YEAR	TEAM	LVL	AGE	W	L	SV	G	GS	IP	H	HR	BB/9	K/9	K	GB%	BABIP
2017	ABQ	AAA	22	0	0	0	3	2	10	8	2	0.0	16.2	18	53%	.353
2017	COL	MLB	22	11	7	0	29	29	162	174	25	2.7	8.2	147	47%	.316
2018	COL	MLB	23	14	11	0	33	33	196	179	24	2.6	10.6	230	48%	.312
2019	COL	MLB	24	12	5	0	28	28	174	174	29	1.8	9.1	175	50%	.304
2020	COL	MLB	25	10	9	0	26	26	161	176	23	2.6	9.7	172	49%	.339

Comparables: Lucas Giolito, Phil Hughes, Luis Severino

What a player deserved is at the heart at a lot of advanced metrics. When it comes to DRA, the notion of what is deserved rests on a player's expected contribution to each play. No play is made in isolation, and no player should get the entirety of the outcome credited to them.

How, then, should we process the fact that DRA considers Márquez to have been one of the top 20 starters in baseball once again? It is clear that he pitched more or less as well at home as he did on the road in terms of strikeouts, walks, and even home runs. It is also clear that he gave up two and a half more runs per nine innings in Colorado than he did everywhere else, and that over 150 points of BABIP separated his home performance from away.

Should we then consider Márquez to have been essentially the same pitcher regardless of whether he was in Denver or not? Should we think that Márquez was just as good as he was in 2018 (slightly better, in fact), when all the talk was of his mastering Coors? We probably should, and yet even with all the context the stats provide, it's hard to believe it. Knowing that he deserved certain results isn't quite the same as understanding that in an alternative universe, there's a Márquez that repeated his 2018 ERA, just as there was a Márquez last season that struggled badly at Coors.

When we get to the real outliers, we just have to try that little bit harder to accept what the underlying stats are telling us. It is one thing to say that a player gave up a few extra home runs and just got unlucky. It's another to believe that Márquez allowed almost twice as many runs as he deserved to at home based on his own expected contribution.

Or maybe this isn't difficult to accept at all. Maybe the issue is simply that Márquez made a seemingly convincing case that a good enough starter *could* reliably overcome Coors, and then that case was thoroughly dismissed. The deserved numbers tell us that the Rockies' ace did effectively pitch like one, if not of the very highest quality then certainly of the tier below. What happens after the ball leaves his hand is not in his control, and sometimes we get an unpleasant reminder that Coors, like life, doesn't always give you what you deserve.

YEAR	TEAM	LVL	AGE	WHIP	ERA	DRA	WARP	MPH	FB%	WHF	CSP
2017	ABQ	AAA	22	0.80	2.70	1.00	0.5				
2017	COL	MLB	22	1.38	4.39	5.08	0.9	97.9	65.5	10	53.7
2018	COL	MLB	23	1.20	3.77	3.23	4.7	97.9	54.9	13.4	49.9
2019	COL	MLB	24	1.20	4.76	3.26	4.7	97.7	52.1	13.2	50.5
2020	*COL*	*MLB*	*25*	*1.38*	*4.63*	*4.22*	*2.8*	*97.5*	*57.7*	*12.8*	*52.3*

Colorado Rockies 2020

German Márquez, continued

Pitch Shape vs LHH

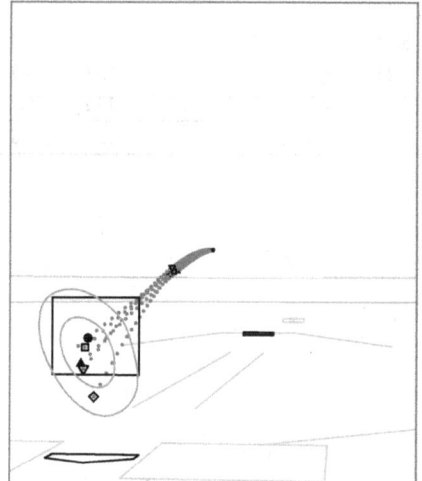

Pitch Shape vs RHH

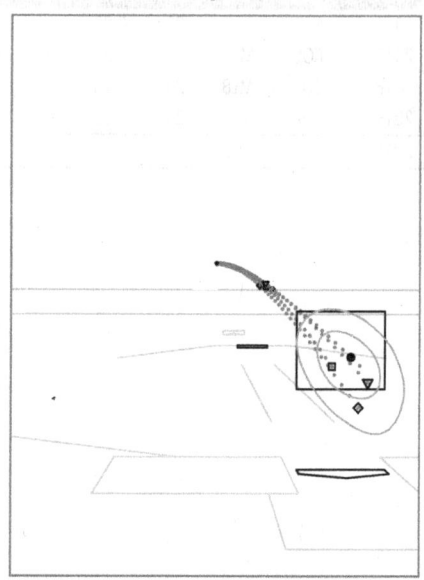

Type	Frequency	Velocity	H Movement	V Movement
● Fastball	40.6%	95.8 [110]	-6.5 [101]	-14.8 [103]
☐ Sinker	11.5%	94.6 [110]	-11.5 [107]	-20.2 [101]
+ Cutter				
▲ Changeup	3.3%	88.2 [111]	-11.9 [97]	-23.3 [112]
✕ Splitter				
▽ Slider	22.4%	87.4 [113]	0.8 [82]	-28.6 [113]
◇ Curveball	22.2%	84.9 [121]	3.1 [82]	-36.3 [124]
⊕ Slow Curveball				
✳ Knuckleball				
▼ Screwball				

Scott Oberg RHP

Born: 03/13/90 Age: 30 Bats: R Throws: R
Height: 6'2" Weight: 203 Origin: Round 15, 2012 Draft (#468 overall)

YEAR	TEAM	LVL	AGE	W	L	SV	G	GS	IP	H	HR	BB/9	K/9	K	GB%	BABIP
2017	COL	MLB	27	0	1	0	66	0	58^1	70	4	3.7	8.5	55	58%	.367
2018	ABQ	AAA	28	1	0	3	13	0	15^1	14	1	1.2	8.2	14	62%	.333
2018	COL	MLB	28	8	1	0	56	0	58^2	45	4	1.8	8.7	57	58%	.270
2019	COL	MLB	29	6	1	5	49	0	56	39	5	3.7	9.3	58	51%	.248
2020	COL	MLB	30	3	3	19	55	0	58	58	8	3.4	9.6	62	52%	.316

Comparables: Kevin Quackenbush, Darren O'Day, Neftalí Feliz

In early August, Oberg finally got his reward for being the best reliever in the Rockies 'pen: He was promoted to closer at the expense of Wade Davis. Two weeks later, his season came to an abrupt end in scary fashion when he was hospitalized with blood clots in his pitching arm. While it was the second time Oberg suffered from a problem with clots, the 29-year-old is confident the underlying cause has now been treated. As long as the issue is truly past, Bud Black desperately needs Oberg in his bullpen. He was the team's highest-leverage option in 2019 even though his run as closer was so quickly curtailed. That status was deserved too, as the right-hander's season ranked as one of the top 10 all-time Rockies pitching seasons by not only ERA, but also DRA-. Regardless of how he is deployed in 2020, it will simply be good to see Oberg back on the mound.

YEAR	TEAM	LVL	AGE	WHIP	ERA	DRA	WARP	MPH	FB%	WHF	CSP
2017	COL	MLB	27	1.61	4.94	4.89	0.2	98.4	56.4	12.2	50.5
2018	ABQ	AAA	28	1.04	1.76	3.36	0.3				
2018	COL	MLB	28	0.97	2.45	3.49	1.0	97.4	55.1	14.7	48.1
2019	COL	MLB	29	1.11	2.25	3.31	1.2	96.1	52.2	13.2	47.2
2020	COL	MLB	30	1.37	4.26	3.97	0.9	96.3	54.1	13.4	48.2

Scott Oberg, continued

Pitch Shape vs LHH

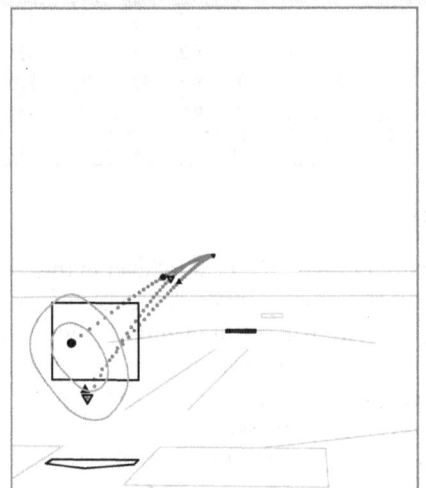

Pitch Shape vs RHH

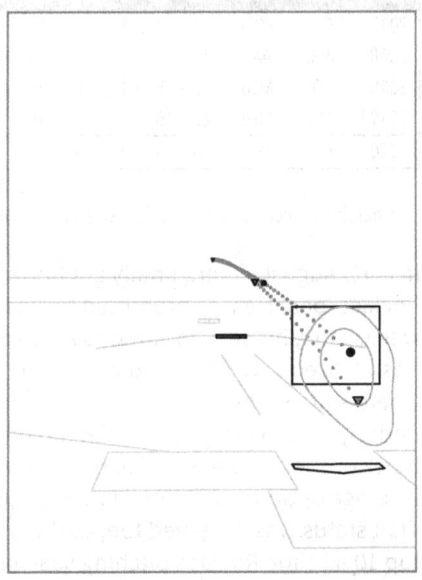

Type	Frequency	Velocity	H Movement	V Movement
● Fastball	52.2%	94.5 [106]	-1.7 [123]	-15 [102]
☐ Sinker				
+ Cutter				
▲ Changeup	4.5%	88.2 [111]	-10.9 [101]	-25.6 [105]
✕ Splitter				
▽ Slider	43.4%	85.9 [106]	5.4 [102]	-33.2 [100]
◇ Curveball				
⊕ Slow Curveball				
✹ Knuckleball				
▼ Screwball				

Antonio Senzatela   RHP
Born: 01/21/95   Age: 25   Bats: R   Throws: R
Height: 6'1"   Weight: 246   Origin: International Free Agent, 2011

YEAR	TEAM	LVL	AGE	W	L	SV	G	GS	IP	H	HR	BB/9	K/9	K	GB%	BABIP
2017	COL	MLB	22	10	5	0	36	20	134²	128	18	3.1	6.8	102	50%	.280
2018	ABQ	AAA	23	3	1	0	8	8	37²	29	1	2.9	10.0	42	48%	.298
2018	COL	MLB	23	6	6	0	23	13	90¹	94	10	3.0	6.9	69	47%	.302
2019	ABQ	AAA	24	1	1	0	7	7	34¹	45	7	2.6	3.1	12	50%	.314
2019	COL	MLB	24	11	11	0	25	25	124²	161	19	4.1	5.5	76	55%	.333
2020	COL	MLB	25	7	9	0	24	24	122	152	18	3.5	5.9	80	52%	.329

Comparables: Zach Eflin, Jake Thompson, Reynaldo López

Living at extremes becomes a fact of life for Colorado starters. Senzatela had dealt admirably with that in his first two major-league seasons, which defied the environment with solid, respectable production. This year, when Coors saw the fifth-most home runs of any park in major-league history, Senzatela also veered towards the extreme in a number of areas. The good: Only three pitchers with as many starts had a higher ground ball rate in 2019. The bad: He also fell behind 3-0 more often than all but one of those starters, and none of them gave up more hits per inning than the young right-hander. Senzatela would be very happy with falling back to the middle ground, as long as the same also happened to his ERA.

YEAR	TEAM	LVL	AGE	WHIP	ERA	DRA	WARP	MPH	FB%	WHF	CSP
2017	COL	MLB	22	1.30	4.68	4.63	1.3	97.4	71.8	7.6	52.2
2018	ABQ	AAA	23	1.09	2.15	2.73	1.2				
2018	COL	MLB	23	1.37	4.38	5.10	0.1	96.6	64.1	8.9	47.5
2019	ABQ	AAA	24	1.60	5.77	5.63	0.4				
2019	COL	MLB	24	1.75	6.71	7.14	-1.9	96.1	63.7	8	48
2020	COL	MLB	25	1.64	5.91	5.19	0.9	96.3	67.6	8.3	50.1

Colorado Rockies 2020

Antonio Senzatela, continued

Pitch Shape vs LHH **Pitch Shape vs RHH**

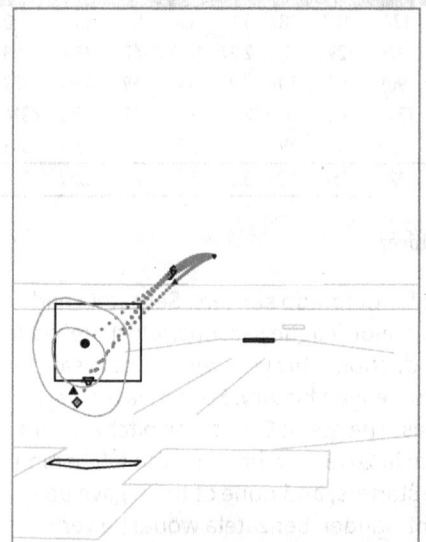 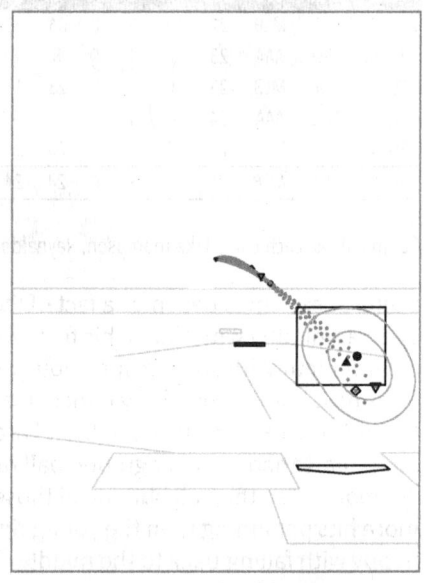

Type	Frequency	Velocity	H Movement	V Movement
● Fastball	63.7%	93.7 [104]	-4.2 [112]	-17.2 [97]
☐ Sinker				
+ Cutter				
▲ Changeup	6.3%	86.8 [105]	-6.3 [123]	-22.9 [113]
✕ Splitter				
▽ Slider	19.8%	84.3 [100]	5.1 [100]	-33.2 [100]
◇ Curveball	10.3%	79 [101]	5.4 [92]	-42.7 [110]
✥ Slow Curveball				
✱ Knuckleball				
▼ Screwball				

Bryan Shaw RHP

Born: 11/08/87 Age: 32 Bats: B Throws: R
Height: 6'1" Weight: 232 Origin: Round 2, 2008 Draft (#73 overall)

YEAR	TEAM	LVL	AGE	W	L	SV	G	GS	IP	H	HR	BB/9	K/9	K	GB%	BABIP
2017	CLE	MLB	29	4	6	3	79	0	76^2	71	5	2.6	8.6	73	57%	.311
2018	COL	MLB	30	4	6	0	61	0	54^2	70	9	4.6	8.9	54	49%	.370
2019	COL	MLB	31	3	2	1	70	0	72	69	12	3.6	7.2	58	50%	.275
2020	COL	MLB	32	2	3	0	50	0	52	55	8	3.7	8.0	46	50%	.308

Comparables: Greg McMichael, Kevin Jepsen, Juan Rincon

The $106 million the Rockies spent on their bullpen two offseasons ago was met with a lot of head-scratching. If one studied their comments for long enough to figure out this mystery, it appeared that they greatly valued durability, as well as the benefit of a pitcher's having an extended period of time in which to adjust to pitching at Coors. Well, Shaw has largely lived up to the durability part; he appeared in another 70 games in 2019. Only Tyler Clippard has made more pitching appearances since Shaw first appeared in the majors in 2011. As for adjusting to Coors, suffice it to say that that these past two seasons have, by a comfortable margin, been the worst of his career. Shaw's got at least one more season to prove that theory right, and likely two: in order for his 2021 option to vest, he just has to appear in 40 games. That's a mark he's topped by more than 20 games every year but his rookie season, when he only arrived in mid-June. Colorado might not be so pleased about that durability after all.

YEAR	TEAM	LVL	AGE	WHIP	ERA	DRA	WARP	MPH	FB%	WHF	CSP
2017	CLE	MLB	29	1.21	3.52	2.73	2.1	96.8	88.2	13.1	48.4
2018	COL	MLB	30	1.79	5.93	4.07	0.5	96.5	84.8	12.5	43.8
2019	COL	MLB	31	1.36	5.38	5.05	0.2	94.8	75.4	11.6	44.7
2020	COL	MLB	32	1.47	4.96	4.54	0.5	94.9	80.9	12.2	44.9

Colorado Rockies 2020

Bryan Shaw, continued

Pitch Shape vs LHH

Pitch Shape vs RHH

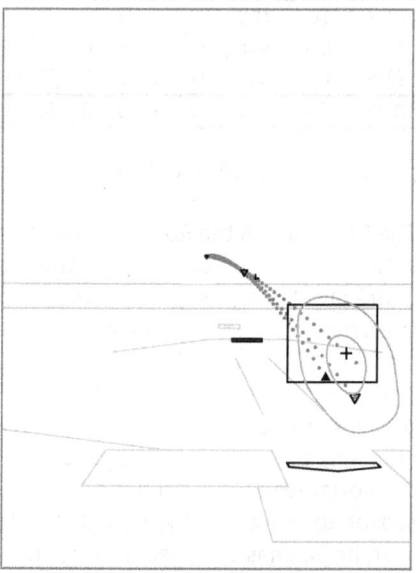

Type	Frequency	Velocity	H Movement	V Movement
● Fastball				
□ Sinker				
+ Cutter	75.3%	92.6 [124]	4 [113]	-21.9 [108]
▲ Changeup	7.5%	84.1 [96]	-5.3 [128]	-28.3 [97]
✕ Splitter				
▽ Slider	17.1%	82.1 [90]	9 [117]	-41.6 [75]
◇ Curveball				
⊕ Slow Curveball				
✱ Knuckleball				
▼ Screwball				

PLAYER COMMENTS WITHOUT GRAPHS

Tyler Nevin 1B
Born: 05/29/97 Age: 23 Bats: R Throws: R
Height: 6'4" Weight: 200 Origin: Round 1, 2015 Draft (#38 overall)

YEAR	TEAM	LVL	AGE	PA	R	2B	3B	HR	RBI	BB	K	SB	CS	AVG/OBP/SLG
2017	BOI	A-	20	30	4	3	0	1	5	0	9	0	1	.233/.233/.433
2017	ASH	A	20	335	45	18	3	7	47	27	56	10	5	.305/.364/.456
2018	LNC	A+	21	417	59	25	1	13	62	34	77	4	3	.328/.386/.503
2019	HFD	AA	22	540	60	26	2	13	61	65	90	6	2	.251/.345/.399
2020	COL	MLB	23	251	26	14	1	7	29	22	58	1	1	.253/.324/.413

Comparables: David Cooper, Rangel Ravelo, Dalton Pompey

Every year, Nevin plays a little more cold corner than hot, making evaluators lukewarm on his chances of being a regular in the majors. Some of that is based on circumstance rather than Nevin's talent, but he's also not a good third baseman, and if he's going to become an everyday player, the bat really needs to heat up. The performance was better than the slash line looks given how difficult it is to hit in the Eastern League. Even with a late-season homer surge, the power has not yet developed enough to make this profile work at first.

YEAR	TEAM	LVL	AGE	PA	DRC+	VORP	BABIP	BRR	FRAA	WARP
2017	BOI	A-	20	30	55	0.1	.300	0.1	3B(3): 0.0, 1B(2): -0.2	-0.1
2017	ASH	A	20	335	133	18.5	.349	1.3	1B(32): 1.6, 3B(23): -2.5	1.8
2018	LNC	A+	21	417	139	15.1	.383	-4.4	1B(67): -0.7, 3B(17): 1.0	1.9
2019	HFD	AA	22	540	120	9.5	.283	1.9	1B(97): 2.8, 3B(12): 0.1	2.4
2020	COL	MLB	23	251	84	2.4	.311	-0.4	1B 1, 3B 0	0.3

Dom Nuñez C

Born: 01/17/95 Age: 25 Bats: L Throws: R
Height: 6'0" Weight: 175 Origin: Round 6, 2013 Draft (#169 overall)

YEAR	TEAM	LVL	AGE	PA	R	2B	3B	HR	RBI	BB	K	SB	CS	AVG/OBP/SLG
2017	HFD	AA	22	364	37	10	1	11	28	53	83	7	1	.202/.335/.354
2018	HFD	AA	23	377	34	12	0	9	42	46	73	8	6	.222/.320/.343
2019	ABQ	AAA	24	257	43	14	1	17	42	35	69	2	0	.244/.362/.559
2019	COL	MLB	24	43	4	3	0	2	4	3	17	0	0	.179/.233/.410
2020	COL	MLB	25	245	25	10	0	8	28	25	72	2	1	.207/.294/.369

Comparables: Bill Sarni, Austin Dean, Jake Smolinski

A premature nickname can be more of a curse than a blessing. Case in point: the Rockies' Twitter account dubbed their 24-year-old catcher 'Bomb Nuñez' when he homered in his very first major-league game. That blew up in their faces over the next month and a half, as Nuñez did nothing but bomb

YEAR	TEAM	P. COUNT	FRM RUNS	BLK RUNS	THRW RUNS	TOT RUNS
2017	HFD	5592	11.6	0.5	0.5	12.3
2018	HFD	9227	6.6	0.7	0.4	7.9
2019	ABQ	9193	5.2	0.1	-0.9	4.3
2019	COL	1637	0.3	0.6	0.0	1.2
2020	COL	9102	3.9	1.4	-0.2	5.1

at the plate. On the very final day of the season, he ensured that the moniker-making homer was not his only blast of 2019 and helped Colorado to finish a single game ahead of the basement-dwelling Padres in the process. The social media team wasted no time in rolling out the nickname again. As long as it doesn't catch on when he strikes out, they've probably gotten away with this one.

YEAR	TEAM	LVL	AGE	PA	DRC+	VORP	BABIP	BRR	FRAA	WARP
2017	HFD	AA	22	364	93	15.2	.238	0.0	C(88): 12.2	2.7
2018	HFD	AA	23	377	90	6.3	.257	-1.0	C(70): 5.8	1.7
2019	ABQ	AAA	24	257	112	19.2	.269	-0.3	C(60): 7.6	2.3
2019	COL	MLB	24	43	74	0.8	.238	1.0	C(14): 0.9	0.3
2020	COL	MLB	25	245	70	1.6	.268	-0.4	C 6	0.7

Ryan Vilade SS

Born: 02/18/99 Age: 21 Bats: R Throws: R
Height: 6'2" Weight: 194 Origin: Round 2, 2017 Draft (#48 overall)

YEAR	TEAM	LVL	AGE	PA	R	2B	3B	HR	RBI	BB	K	SB	CS	AVG/OBP/SLG
2017	GJR	RK	18	146	23	3	2	5	21	27	31	5	5	.308/.438/.496
2018	ASH	A	19	533	77	20	4	5	44	49	96	17	13	.274/.353/.368
2019	LNC	A+	20	587	92	27	10	12	71	56	95	24	7	.303/.367/.466
2020	COL	MLB	21	251	23	11	2	4	23	23	56	4	2	.238/.314/.348

Comparables: Gavin Lux, Daniel Robertson, Carlos Rivero

Vilade's offensive development continued smoothly at High-A, where he demonstrated a strong all-fields approach with power to boot. The road has been a little more bumpy defensively, where his 37 errors speak to the issues he's had throwing the ball. Vilade spent more time at third base as the season went on and could yet develop into a plus defender given his athleticism. He's also an excellent baserunner despite not having top-end speed. The components are all here for an above-average player on all sides of the ball, and Vilade has given every indication that he'll be able to realize that potential.

YEAR	TEAM	LVL	AGE	PA	DRC+	VORP	BABIP	BRR	FRAA	WARP
2017	GJR	RK	18	146	130	14.0	.378	0.4	SS(30): -2.1	0.6
2018	ASH	A	19	533	114	25.8	.333	-1.9	SS(116): -6.3	2.1
2019	LNC	A+	20	587	118	33.5	.342	2.5	SS(82): -4.0, 3B(46): -4.3	2.6
2020	COL	MLB	21	251	79	1.2	.302	0.0	SS -2, 3B 0	-0.1

Colorado Rockies 2020

Ben Bowden LHP
Born: 10/21/94 Age: 25 Bats: L Throws: L
Height: 6'4" Weight: 235 Origin: Round 2, 2016 Draft (#45 overall)

YEAR	TEAM	LVL	AGE	W	L	SV	G	GS	IP	H	HR	BB/9	K/9	K	GB%	BABIP
2018	ASH	A	23	3	0	0	15	0	15^1	17	2	2.9	14.7	25	43%	.429
2018	LNC	A+	23	4	2	0	34	0	36^2	35	6	3.7	13.0	53	35%	.337
2019	HFD	AA	24	0	0	20	26	0	25^2	8	1	2.5	14.7	42	38%	.171
2019	ABQ	AAA	24	1	3	1	22	0	26	29	4	5.9	12.8	37	34%	.379
2020	COL	MLB	25	1	1	0	11	0	12	13	2	3.4	12.1	16	38%	.365

Comparables: Paul Fry, Andrew Vasquez, James Pazos

Bowden appeared to be racing to the majors over the first half of the season. After giving up three runs in his third appearance at Double-A, he recorded 23 consecutive scoreless appearances with 39 strikeouts and just five walks to practically force the Rockies to promote him to Albuquerque. The second-round pick failed to bend the team to his will once he got there, as he struggled with control and proved far more hittable. He also came to wider prominence for the wrong reason, surrendering the Futures Game-tying home run to Rangers prospect Sam Huff. DRA still considered Bowden an above-average pitcher, and with three pitches, including a sinker with plenty of run, he is better-equipped than many relievers to deal with life in Colorado. His major-league bow isn't far off.

YEAR	TEAM	LVL	AGE	WHIP	ERA	DRA	WARP	MPH	FB%	WHF	CSP
2018	ASH	A	23	1.43	3.52	3.64	0.2				
2018	LNC	A+	23	1.36	4.17	3.48	0.6				
2019	HFD	AA	24	0.58	1.05	1.94	0.8				
2019	ABQ	AAA	24	1.77	5.88	4.49	0.4				
2020	COL	MLB	25	1.47	5.13	4.67	0.1				

Riley Pint   RHP

Born: 11/06/97   Age: 22   Bats: R   Throws: R
Height: 6'5"   Weight: 225   Origin: Round 1, 2016 Draft (#4 overall)

YEAR	TEAM	LVL	AGE	W	L	SV	G	GS	IP	H	HR	BB/9	K/9	K	GB%	BABIP
2017	ASH	A	19	2	11	0	22	22	93	96	3	5.7	7.6	79	60%	.325
2018	BOI	A-	20	0	2	0	3	3	8	4	0	10.1	9.0	8	47%	.235
2019	ASH	A	21	0	1	0	21	3	17²	12	0	15.8	11.7	23	50%	.316
2020	COL	MLB	22	2	2	0	33	0	35	34	5	4.5	7.2	28	51%	.285

Comparables: Sal Romano, Nate Adcock, Tyrell Jenkins

Saying that Pint has control problems is like saying the Titanic had iceberg problems. It's *technically* accurate while barely scratching the surface of the issue. Pint walked an astounding 31 of the 98 batters he faced for Asheville before going down with yet another injury, this time a shoulder strain. Any evaluator will tell you that Pint's stuff is so electric that his ceiling is as high as that of almost any pitching prospect in the game. At this point, however, the possibility that the control issues sink his career before he even reaches the majors looms disturbingly large underneath the veneer of that gaudy stuff.

YEAR	TEAM	LVL	AGE	WHIP	ERA	DRA	WARP	MPH	FB%	WHF	CSP
2017	ASH	A	19	1.67	5.42	5.67	-0.4				
2018	BOI	A-	20	1.62	1.12	5.39	0.0				
2019	ASH	A	21	2.43	8.66	7.50	-0.6				
2020	COL	MLB	22	1.48	4.90	4.99	0.2				

Ryan Rolison LHP

Born: 07/11/97 Age: 22 Bats: R Throws: L
Height: 6'2" Weight: 195 Origin: Round 1, 2018 Draft (#22 overall)

YEAR	TEAM	LVL	AGE	W	L	SV	G	GS	IP	H	HR	BB/9	K/9	K	GB%	BABIP
2018	GJR	RK	20	0	1	0	9	9	29	15	2	2.5	10.6	34	66%	.200
2019	ASH	A	21	2	1	0	3	3	14^2	8	0	1.2	8.6	14	40%	.216
2019	LNC	A+	21	6	7	0	22	22	116^1	129	22	2.9	9.1	118	46%	.320
2020	COL	MLB	22	2	2	0	33	0	35	36	6	3.5	7.5	29	42%	.288

Comparables: Josh Rogers, Devin Smeltzer, Scott Diamond

Rolison came into the season as BP's top pitching prospect in the Rockies organization and left with more questions than answers. While his four-pitch mix and high degree of polish helped him make short work of Low-A, the same couldn't be said of his lengthier stint at the level above. The command wavered frequently, and the underlying stuff simply didn't flash enough to compensate for it. His curveball leads the way when the command is on, but with the fastball struggling to get out of the low 90s and a slider and change that have a long way to go to catch up with the curve, more than a little extra polish is needed to make this package play at the higher levels.

YEAR	TEAM	LVL	AGE	WHIP	ERA	DRA	WARP	MPH	FB%	WHF	CSP
2018	GJR	RK	20	0.79	1.86	0.65	1.7				
2019	ASH	A	21	0.68	0.61	2.43	0.5				
2019	LNC	A+	21	1.44	4.87	4.61	0.6				
2020	COL	MLB	22	1.41	4.76	5.02	0.2				

LINEOUTS

Hitters

HITTER	POS	TEAM	LVL	AGE	PA	R	2B	3B	HR	RBI	BB	K	SB	CS	AVG/OBP/SLG	DRC+	WARP
Julio Carreras	3B	GJR	Rk+	19	307	51	14	8	5	38	25	63	14	8	.294/.369/.466	115	1.8
Yonathan Daza	LF	COL	MLB	25	105	7	1	1	0	3	7	21	1	0	.206/.257/.237	60	0.0
	LF	ABQ	AAA	25	418	67	30	4	11	48	25	52	12	9	.364/.404/.548	122	2.8
Eddy Diaz	SS	GJR	Rk+	19	177	32	12	3	0	10	8	33	20	9	.331/.366/.440	131	1.3
Brenton Doyle	RF	GJR	Rk+	21	215	42	11	3	8	33	31	47	17	3	.383/.477/.611	198	3.1
Josh Fuentes	3B	COL	MLB	26	56	8	1	0	3	7	1	20	1	0	.218/.232/.400	73	-0.1
	3B	ABQ	AAA	26	437	66	23	2	17	64	25	118	1	1	.254/.298/.448	67	0.8
Chris Iannetta	C	COL	MLB	36	164	20	10	0	6	21	18	54	0	0	.222/.311/.417	82	0.0
Grant Lavigne	1B	ASH	A	19	526	52	19	0	7	64	68	129	8	9	.236/.347/.327	87	-0.5
Roberto Ramos	1B	ABQ	AAA	24	503	77	27	0	30	105	61	141	0	1	.309/.400/.580	124	1.4
Mark Reynolds	1B	COL	MLB	35	162	13	7	0	4	20	22	57	2	0	.170/.290/.311	66	-0.7
Aaron Schunk	3B	BOI	A-	21	192	31	12	2	6	23	14	25	4	1	.306/.370/.503	138	2.2
Eric Stamets	SS	CLE	MLB	27	48	4	1	0	0	2	5	24	0	0	.049/.149/.073	38	-0.3
	SS	COH	AAA	27	327	40	10	5	6	38	27	83	14	1	.244/.312/.373	65	0.2
Michael Toglia	1B	BOI	A-	20	176	25	7	0	9	26	28	45	1	1	.248/.369/.483	132	0.6
Terrin Vavra	SS	ASH	A	22	453	79	32	1	10	52	62	62	18	9	.318/.409/.489	152	4.0

A 2017 international signee, **Julio Carreras** made some noise in the Dominican Summer League and continued to do so in his stateside debut. There's speed, athleticism, and, if he can iron out his approach at the plate, an exciting future ahead. He's got plenty of time to do it. ⚾ **Yonathan Daza**'s run at the PCL batting title was a promising chapter in his quest to be more than just a fourth outfielder. The next installment may prove to be rather more challenging, as he needs to pass several other options on a team that rarely hands rookies a starring role. ⚾ **Eddy Diaz** loves to run, but he found catchers in the Pioneer League to be a tougher assignment than those he had succeeded against at an 86 percent rate in the Dominican Republic. His blazing speed and contact skills still helped him to excel at the plate before a knee injury cut short his season. ⚾ Fourth-rounder **Brenton Doyle** couldn't be stopped in the Pioneer League. That even proved to be the case when a foul ball into the dugout broke his cheekbone: Doyle was only out for three weeks and marched to a batting title upon his return. ⚾ Now that the upper levels of pro ball have silenced his bat, you'd be hard-pressed to convince people **Josh Fuentes** wasn't a generic OOTP regen, particularly considering the suspicious proximity between his pro debut and the retirement of namesake Brian. ⚾ They say you can't ever go home again, but as **Chris Iannetta** proved, it's really easy to go home. You just can't ever be young or hopeful or happy ever again. ⚾ Following up on an incredible debut in Rookie ball, **Grant Lavigne** acted like somebody else entirely with Asheville. He needs to start taking what he gets and turning it into something other than ground balls, as he can't even fake it anywhere but first base. Oh Grant. Why'd you have to go and make things so complicated? ⓥ That **Roberto Ramos**' near-1.000 OPS at Triple-A was only good for a 124 DRC+ spoke volumes about both the swing-and-miss in his game and what the major-league ball has done to the Triple-A run environment. ⓥ If you weren't already convinced that **Mark Reynolds** is blind, his 2019 stat line aught to prove it. The Chandrayaan-2 made better contact. ⓥ Schunk is one of the words that appears when Batman hits a villain. Reports that the same happens when a ball hits **Aaron Schunk**'s bat have yet to be confirmed. ⓥ **Eric Stamets** spent the first two weeks of the season filling in for Francisco Lindor, which would be a little like trying to replace *Veep*'s Julia Louis-Dreyfuss with baseball's Eric Stamets. ⓥ The Rockies drafted switch-hitting slugger **Michael Toglia** 23rd overall and signed him for $2.7 million. Turning Colorado down for UCLA as a 35th-rounder back in 2016 was the right call. ⓥ Remarkably, **Terrin Vavra** is not the protagonist of an interstellar sci-fi novel. If one wanted to make the case he is from another planet, however, his numbers with Asheville would be an excellent starting point.

Pitchers

PITCHER	TEAM	LVL	AGE	W	L	SV	G	GS	IP	H	HR	BB/9	K/9	K	GB%	WHIP	ERA	DRA	WARP
Ryan Castellani	ABQ	AAA	23	2	5	0	10	10	43^1	54	14	6.2	9.8	47	46%	1.94	8.31	8.02	-0.5
Mike Dunn	COL	MLB	34	1	0	0	28	0	17^2	17	4	3.1	7.6	15	41%	1.30	7.13	4.24	0.2
Rico Garcia	HFD	AA	25	8	2	0	13	13	68	41	4	3.0	11.5	87	49%	0.94	1.85	2.95	1.7
	ABQ	AAA	25	2	4	0	13	13	61^1	77	14	4.1	7.5	51	37%	1.71	6.90	5.95	0.5
	COL	MLB	25	0	1	0	2	1	6	9	3	7.5	3.0	2	44%	2.33	10.50	7.29	-0.1
Ashton Goudeau	HFD	AA	26	3	3	0	16	16	78^1	60	4	1.4	10.5	91	45%	0.92	2.07	3.18	1.7
Alexander Guillen	HFD	AA	23	2	2	1	37	0	76^2	50	4	2.5	10.7	91	44%	0.93	1.53	2.50	2.0
Joe Harvey	ABQ	AAA	27	0	1	1	9	0	8^2	12	5	5.2	10.4	10	21%	1.96	10.38	7.88	-0.1
	SWB	AAA	27	0	1	9	22	0	26	15	4	5.2	13.2	38	23%	1.15	3.12	2.80	0.9
	NYA	MLB	27	1	0	0	9	0	10	11	1	6.3	9.9	11	48%	1.80	4.50	5.45	0.0
	COL	MLB	27	0	0	0	9	0	8	7	2	6.8	6.8	6	44%	1.62	5.62	7.87	-0.2
Mitchell Kilkenny	GJR	Rk+	22	2	3	0	12	12	42	44	3	2.1	7.9	37	56%	1.29	4.50	4.21	0.9
Tyler Kinley	NWO	AAA	28	0	1	2	14	0	15^2	4	1	4.0	10.9	19	36%	0.70	1.72	1.76	0.7
	MIA	MLB	28	3	1	1	52	0	49^1	43	5	6.6	8.4	46	39%	1.60	3.65	5.84	-0.3
Justin Lawrence	HFD	AA	24	0	4	0	30	0	26^2	35	1	6.8	8.8	26	51%	2.06	8.77	7.75	-1.0
	ABQ	AAA	24	1	1	0	8	0	10^1	12	3	7.8	5.2	6	53%	2.03	8.71	7.04	-0.1
Harrison Musgrave	ABQ	AAA	27	0	2	0	21	1	24	51	5	4.5	8.6	23	41%	2.62	10.12	10.41	-1.0
	COL	MLB	27	0	0	0	10	0	10	9	0	6.3	10.8	12	25%	1.60	3.60	4.48	0.1
Seunghwan Oh	COL	MLB	36	3	1	0	21	0	18^1	29	6	2.9	7.9	16	38%	1.91	9.33	6.27	-0.2
Wes Parsons	GWN	AAA	26	2	3	4	27	0	56^2	58	1	3.3	8.6	54	57%	1.39	2.86	4.09	1.2
	ATL	MLB	26	1	2	0	17	0	15^1	11	2	7.6	7.0	12	45%	1.57	3.52	6.77	-0.2
	COL	MLB	26	0	0	0	15	0	19^1	21	4	7.4	6.5	14	48%	1.91	6.98	7.61	-0.5
James Pazos	ABQ	AAA	28	1	3	1	39	0	44	69	8	4.7	8.6	42	48%	2.09	8.80	6.91	-0.3
	LEH	AAA	28	0	1	2	7	0	7^1	8	0	8.6	4.9	4	42%	2.05	6.14	6.96	-0.1
	COL	MLB	28	0	0	0	12	0	10^1	7	1	3.5	8.7	10	60%	1.06	1.74	4.62	0.1
Chris Rusin	HFD	AA	32	1	0	0	3	0	7	8	0	3.9	6.4	5	39%	1.57	5.14	5.58	-0.1
	ABQ	AAA	32	3	4	0	22	10	65^2	83	7	2.9	5.8	42	55%	1.58	4.93	4.50	1.3
	COL	MLB	32	0	0	0	2	0	1	5	1	9.0	0.0	0	12%	6.00	36.00	8.43	0.0
Antonio Santos	LNC	A+	22	3	6	0	18	18	99^1	116	11	1.6	8.7	96	42%	1.35	4.35	5.17	-0.2
	HFD	AA	22	3	3	0	8	8	45^2	47	3	2.0	8.7	44	41%	1.25	4.93	5.09	-0.1
Jesus Tinoco	ABQ	AAA	24	3	1	1	29	0	34	33	4	4.8	6.1	23	55%	1.50	3.97	4.15	0.7
	COL	MLB	24	0	3	1	24	0	36	36	12	5.5	7.0	28	44%	1.61	4.75	6.83	-0.6

A solid AFL showing in 2018 did enough to earn **Ryan Castellani** the call to Triple-A. There he got lit up, then sidelined with bone fragments in his elbow. He returned to the AFL, where an excellent ERA masked more mixed performance. If his work in Arizona impressed the team again, a major-league debut is imminent. ⓧ Pretty much all you need to know about **Mike Dunn**'s unsightly Rockies career is that now all three of his corresponding Annual comments mention the phrase "sunk cost." ⓘ An utterly dominant half-season at Double-A Hartford must feel a very long way off now for **Rico Garcia**. The 30th-round pick joined a long list of pitchers who would rather they hadn't toured the PCL and capped that off by getting crushed in his major-league debut. ⓘ **Ashton Goudeau** just recorded his best season as a professional pitcher thanks to an ERA approaching 2.00. Drafted way back in 2012, it's been a long time coming—and at 26 and only in Double-A, the Rockies may spend a few years yet waiting for Goudeau. ⓘ **Alexander Guillen** dazzled in a multi-inning relief role throughout the minor league season and maintained his dominance in the Arizona Fall League. ⓘ **Joe Harvey**'s results have been anything but average. A string of exceptionally good ratios was snapped by a rough introduction to the majors and an even more unpleasant trip to Albuquerque after his trade to Colorado. As a major-leaguer, he'd settle for being just an average Joe. ⓘ After leading Michigan all the way to the College World Series, Wolverines ace **Karl Kauffmann** fell at the final hurdle in the decider. His next challenge is to prove he can complement his lively sinker with enough secondaries to stick at the back end of the rotation. ⓘ Crushed? Sure. Mauled? It works. Trampled? Possibly. Spontaneously combusted? Plausible, if unconventional. Electrocuted? Back to the drawing board. **Mitchell Kilkenny** survived Tommy John surgery and made a solid pro debut, but every time he gets lit up, the only saving grace will be that some of Kenny's myriad *South Park* demises are just not going to fit in a headline. ⓘ You've heard of the Kinsey Scale, yeah? Well here's the Kinley Scale: it's just **Tyler Kinley**'s walk rate, and it ranges from 14 to 16 percent. ⓘ An aggressive assignment didn't work for sidearmer **Justin Lawrence**, as his command disappeared, along with the high-90s heat from his unusual slot. ⓘ A long-time Rays' farmhand, **José Mujica**, was finally on the front step of the majors in 2019 when Tommy John opened the door and tossed him back so hard he landed in Colorado. ⓘ When you pitch in the Rockies organization, posting a near-5.00 ERA on the road isn't ideal. It wouldn't have mattered regardless for **Harrison Musgrave**, who was attempting to offset an 11.21 ERA at home. ⓘ A common convention in video games is for the difficult boss of an early level to return as a normal enemy in some later stage. The idea is to feel empowering for the player, but when you consider **Seunghwan Oh**, it's kind of depressing from the boss' point of view. ⓘ The Rockies took a gamble on **Wes Parsons** after he showed decent run prevention skills in Atlanta's org. That didn't pay off, as Parson's peripherals got the best of him in Colorado. ⓘ **James Pazos** was one of the worst relievers in the minors before the Phillies designated him for assignment and one of the worst relievers in the minors after the Rockies picked him up, but gave up just one run in 12 games when he was recalled in September. Small sample size can be a wonderful thing. ⓘ **Chris Rusin** allowed six of the nine major-league batters he faced to reach base and wasn't all that much better in the minors. Somehow, that resulted in his finishing the minor-league season in the rotation for the first time since 2016. ⚾ **Antonio Santos** has a playable fastball and a bunch of unremarkable secondaries. His delivery screams "reliever," but the Rockies keep whispering "no" in response. Maybe that'll change this year. ⚾ **Jesus Tinoco** pitched entirely out of the bullpen, but maintained a five-pitch starter's repertoire. Results suggest he might be better off focusing on just two or three of those pitches.

Rockies Prospects

The State of the System
Well, this de-escalated quickly. There's some interesting relief arms, and intriguing low minors guys, but the Rockies system is about as thin as the air up there now.

The Top Ten

--------- ★ ★ ★ *2020 Top 101 Prospect* **#56** ★ ★ ★ ---------

1 Brendan Rodgers SS OFP: 55 ETA: 2019
Born: 08/09/96 Age: 23 Bats: R Throws: R Height: 6'0" Weight: 180
Origin: Round 1, 2015 Draft (#3 overall)

The Report: Rodgers started out the year by torching the Pacific Coast League. Yes, it was in Albuquerque, and yes it was with the major league rabbit ball, but it still quelled some of the concerns you might have had after two just okay seasons in Double-A—and Hartford is far from a pitcher's park itself. He blitzed his way to the majors where he had some initial struggles, although some of those can no doubt be chalked up to the right labrum tear that ended his season in June. It's unknown exactly how he will come back from a fairly major surgery. It might force him to the right side of the infield, but he was already the third-best shortstop glove on the roster behind Trevor Story and Garrett Hampson. And that won't matter if the bat plays to its potential in the majors.

That's still an open question, though. Rodgers has plus raw power and an above-average hit projection. It's not an easy, loose swing, but he shows solid barrel control. He has just never developed enough of an approach against offspeed to consistently put himself in position to do damage. He expands when behind and can be overly aggressive generally, something major league arms were able to exploit during his debut. When he's right, you can dream on a .270, 25-home-run middle infielder—before the Coors boost—with a solid enough glove, but we aren't living in dreams anymore with the 23-year-old Rodgers, and the major league reality is a bit more complicated now.

Variance: Higher than you'd like. There remain questions about the hit tool and approach, and he's had some durability issues. A labrum tear is a non-trivial injury for a hitter as well.

Colorado Rockies 2020

Ben Carsley's Fantasy Take: It's crazy to think that I just turned 30, yet this is the 45th year in a row I've written about Brendan Rodgers: Fantasy Prospect. It's true that Rodgers is not the potential fantasy franchise savior we once saw visions of back in, say, 2016. It's also true that he is as prime a prospect fatigue candidate as I can perhaps ever recall. Just because his ceiling isn't "Carlos Correa at Coors" doesn't mean Rodgers can't help your squad in very short order. A well-rounded infielder in Coors is always going to be of supreme interest to us. Thirty-homer middle infielders aren't as in short supply as they were a decade ago, but they're still mighty nice to own.

2. Ryan Rolison   LHP   OFP: 55   ETA: 2020-21
Born: 07/11/97   Age: 22   Bats: R   Throws: L   Height: 6'2"   Weight: 195
Origin: Round 1, 2018 Draft (#22 overall)

The Report: The Rockies' first-round pick of the 2018 draft, Rolison needed just three starts at Low-A Asheville (14 2/3 IP, 0.61 ERA, 14 K) before earning a promotion to pitcher-unfriendly Lancaster of the High-A California League. The home confines weren't cozy for the lefty, as he posted a 6.06 ERA and opponents hit for a .320 BA in 65 1/3 innings pitched (13 starts). On the road, however, Rolison limited opponents to a .215 BA, struck out 57 batters, and held a 3.35 ERA in 51 IP over nine starts. The 22-year-old left-hander utilizes plus-athleticism and a controlled delivery to command his low-90's fastball, a developing low-80s changeup, and a stellar curveball that can also bump into the low 80s.

Rolison fields his position well, demonstrates good poise, and generally works quickly when on the mound. His game is similar to Barry Zito's in that he'll compete with a well-executed arsenal of quality pitches, rather than overpowering stuff. He profiles long term as a middle-of-the-rotation starting pitcher, but his versatility and advanced pitching acumen would allow him to contribute from a bullpen role as soon as 2020.

Variance: Medium. The low-90's fastball puts added importance on the offspeed offerings, pitch command, and overall execution.

Ben Carsley's Fantasy Take: Every year we struggle to make fantasy writeups for Rockies pitchers interesting. The short answer remains that you should stay away from 99.99 percent of them, Rolison included. However, in very deep leagues, Rolison has some potential utility as a SP5/6 or streamer you may want to occasionally start on the road. That's not worth rostering at present in most formats, but if your league generally sees 250-plus prospects owned, Rolison should be among them.

3. Ryan Vilade   SS   OFP: 55   ETA: 2021
Born: 02/18/99   Age: 21   Bats: R   Throws: R   Height: 6'2"   Weight: 194
Origin: Round 2, 2017 Draft (#48 overall)

The Report: After a slow start to the 2019 season—Vilade hit .250 in April and May—the 20-year-old infielder slashed .330 and hit all but one of his 12 home runs in his final 80 games at High-A Lancaster. He has a relatively flat stroke, but stays inside the ball well and generates consistent hard contact to all fields. He ultimately led the California League with 10 triples, which along with his 27 doubles—fifth most—and 24 stolen bases, showcase his natural strength and athleticism. At 6-foot-2 and 195-pounds, he's demonstrated adequate range and ability as a shortstop, but appears best-suited for the hot corner, where he played 46 games in 2019. He prefers to throw from a low, side-arm slot, enabling a quick release, but also affecting the carry and accuracy on longer throws, contributing to his 37 errors in 128 games last season. Vilade's combination of advanced skills and raw athleticism set a high-floor for the 20-year-old prospect. The ceiling may be an all-star caliber, five-tool third baseman.

Variance: Medium. The combo of baseball skills and raw tools is exciting, but he's just 20-years-old and will need to continue to adapt to the better competition.

Ben Carsley's Fantasy Take: I have a long and troubled history of overrating Rockies infield prospects, but I just can't help myself; I really like Vilade. I have some concerns about him sticking at third base–especially if the Rockies decide to commit to the bold team-building strategy of, uh, not trading their best player–but I'm pretty convinced he's going to hit. Add in plus power and enough athleticism to swipe 10-plus bags a year, and you've got a mighty well-rounded fantasy player. Now imagine that package in Coors! I'll be fighting with Bret to try and get Vilade on the Top-101.

4. Terrin Vavra SS   OFP: 50   ETA: 2021-22
Born: 05/12/97   Age: 23   Bats: L   Throws: R   Height: 6'1"   Weight: 185
Origin: Round 3, 2018 Draft (#96 overall)

The Report: Vavra is a polished offensive contributor with enough glove to stick up the middle. In his first full professional season, he showed good control of the zone and the barrel, with a simple, relatively flat swing plane that hit line drives to all fields. There is some pull-side power in the profile, although almost all of Vavra's 2019 pop came at home with the short right field porch in Asheville. Given his size and swing, the power is more likely to play in the 10-15 home run range, albeit along with a potentially plus hit tool. On the dirt, Vavra is rangy enough for shortstop, but his arm strength might limit him to the right side of the infield.

Variance: Medium. The advanced hit tool should let Vavra carve out a fairly quick path to the majors, but he has limited pro experience and may not stick on the left side of the infield.

Ben Carsley's Fantasy Take: As you can probably glean from the writeup above, Vavra is a better real life prospect than a fantasy one. If he stays in this organization, he's likely to be a utility infielder buried behind more talented options. If he leaves the organization, well, half of his games won't come at Coors. Either way, it's tough to see Vavra as anything more than an accumulator. Given his modest ceiling and that he's not even knocking on the door right now, it's tough to consider him even a top-200 dynasty prospect.

5 Sam Hilliard   OF   OFP: 50   ETA: 2019
Born: 02/21/94   Age: 26   Bats: L   Throws: L   Height: 6'5"   Weight: 238
Origin: Round 15, 2015 Draft (#437 overall)

The Report: Hilliard has always looked like a player who should hit for more power than he has as a pro. When you consider that he's built like a football player and has played his home games in Asheville, Lancaster, and Hartford, you'd have expected a season like his 2019 before now. Yes, it's Albuquerque and Coors, but 40 bombs is 40 bombs. Hilliard has some fairly obvious warts to the profile. The swing has some length and stiffness to it, and he's struggled left-on-left. He looked a bit shorter to the ball in the majors, but there's still some swing-and-miss in the zone, especially if you can elevate above his hands, due to a steep swing path.

There's some good stuff here that might be less obvious too. Despite his size, he's a sneaky athlete, an average runner with a big arm who can hack it in center a couple days a week. Hilliard is also a smart baserunner, and he has an idea of what to take his huge hacks at. This feels like the kind of profile the Rockies give too many at-bats to, as he's more of a long-side platoon outfielder, but Hilliard is major-league-ready and no mere lumbering corner slugger. He will hit some majestic bombs playing in Coors too, and that's always fun.

Variance: Low. He's probably not going to hit .260 long term in the majors, but there's enough pop and athleticism to make him a useful major leaguer of some sort.

Ben Carsley's Fantasy Take: If you're going to be a platoon player with pop, there's no better organization for you to be with than the Colorado Rockies. Hilliard probably *should* only be a fourth outfielder or second-division starter, but his power could make him usable in deeper leagues if he finds himself getting more plate appearances than his skill level and ceiling would suggest he should. He's more of an NL Only bet at this point, but a potentially worthwhile one.

6 Michael Toglia   1B   OFP: 50   ETA: 2021-22
Born: 08/16/98   Age: 21   Bats: B   Throws: L   Height: 6'5"   Weight: 226
Origin: Round 1, 2019 Draft (#23 overall)

The Report: A switch-hitting power threat from both sides of the plate, Toglia's big junior season for UCLA stamped him as a first-round pick despite the defensive limitations in the profile. He's played a fair bit of corner outfield and has plenty of arm for right field, but has primarily played first base as a pro so far. That's going to put a lot of pressure on his bat, but there's plus bat speed and plenty of raw pop to carry the weight of the cold corner. Toglia is tall with long levers in his swing, so there may be swing-and-miss in the zone, but he knows what to swing at and profiles as an everyday Three True Outcomes corner bat with potential 30+ bombs in the majors.

Variance: Medium. The bat should play, but we haven't seen him extensively with wood against better competition yet, and if the offensive profile slides even a bit, it's a tough path to bench bat given the defensive limitations.

Ben Carsley's Fantasy Take: Bret Sayre come get your mans. All jokes about my Internet Dad's affinity for first basemen aside, I like Toglia more than lots of other first-base-only bats. The bat speed checks out, he might offer just enough defensive versatility to eke out extra playing time, and the power upside is high. Toglia isn't a top-101 dynasty prospect–or even terribly close to it–but if you're in the thirdish round of your supplemental draft, you could do worse.

7 Aaron Schunk 3B   OFP: 50 ETA: 2021-22
Born: 07/24/97 Age: 22 Bats: R Throws: R Height: 6'2" Weight: 205
Origin: Round 2, 2019 Draft (#62 overall)

The Report: Schunk won the John Olerud Award for best two-way college player, but his future is on the position player side. He added a bunch of game power his junior year and it should carry over to wood bats, as he will show off plus raw to all fields. He's not a mere corner masher either, as there's a potential above-average hit tool in the profile based on his bat speed and present feel for the barrel. At third base, Schunk is athletic with a good first step and solid hands, with plenty of arm for the hot corner. David Lee saw some Austin Riley potential in the profile this Spring, although Schunk is only three months younger than Riley right now.

Variance: Medium. There's a limited pro track record and the power will need to continue to play up the levels given the corner profile.

Ben Carsley's Fantasy Take: Schunk is just one for your watch list at present, but maybe for the first half of it? Maybe underline his name or something?

8 Colton Welker 3B   OFP: 50 ETA: 2020-21
Born: 10/09/97 Age: 22 Bats: R Throws: R Height: 6'1" Weight: 195
Origin: Round 4, 2016 Draft (#110 overall)

The Report: Welker's first season in Double-A was uneven. The raw power is obvious. It's easy—well, not easy—plus from a violent uppercut hack. There's commensurate plus bat speed, but he can get long and tends to be overly aggressive. Welker only really had one mode against Eastern League arms and he could be exploited by more advanced arms even if they didn't have huge stuff. He struggled to adjust to offspeed and tended to pull off breaking stuff. He'd expand with two strikes and couldn't really cut down. When he made contact, the ball went far, but I wonder how much of the raw pop will get into games. You are basically betting on him making adjustments here, and while there's a good pro track record before this year, it's a tough swing to bet on.

I'd feel better about the overall profile if I were more certain he'd stick at third. The frame is rectangular-ish and he struggled coming in on balls, although he has a decent first step and fine lateral range, the arm is just okay at third base, and overall Welker looked more comfortable across the diamond at first. That would make him a right/right first baseman with a fringe hit tool. That's a tough fit.

Variance: High. There's some risk Welker doesn't hit enough to be more than a corner bench bat. If he does adjust to upper minors pitching and develop a better two-strike approach, he could be a solid regular.

Ben Carsley's Fantasy Take: I've historically been pretty high on Welker, but the scouting reports haven't been trending in his favor for 18-or-so months now. It's a very Michael Chavis profile, and while that can be more useful for fantasy than for actual major league teams, it still makes Welker a relatively poor bet to earn a ton of playing time in Coors. I'm stubborn enough that I'm leaving Welker in my top-200 for now, but I admit that at this point you're basically SOL if either the power or the third base eligibility fall by the wayside. (Now that I'm willing to give up on him, he'll absolutely hit .453 this season).

9 **Grant Lavigne 1B**   OFP: 50   ETA: 2022-23
Born: 08/27/99 Age: 20 Bats: L Throws: R Height: 6'4" Weight: 220
Origin: Round 1, 2018 Draft (#42 overall)

The Report: Yet another corner bat with plus raw power and hit tool questions. Lavigne is the youngest of the group, but has also struggled the most with the transition to the pro game and wood bats so far. He gets good hand-hip separation from his leg kick, but can get out of sync and end up cutting off some of that prodigious raw power due to poor quality of contact. He was at times swinging to stay afloat against South Atlantic League stuff this year, which was a somewhat aggressive assignment for a cold-weather prep bat. Lavigne also struggled with spin, but then there would be an at-bat here or there that he would just swat with a big uppercut and watch the baseball soar. It may take some time for the bat to click, and it might never click, but there's big power upside here. Lavigne is a below-average runner, but athletic enough, not a base clogger or anything, though he's still raw at first base. That should come with reps, and the profile is going to depend far more on the bat than the glove anyway.

Variance: High. Lavigne struggled in his initial full-season assignment and will need to translate his big raw power into games to make it as a starting first baseman. This one is going to take some time to play out too.

Ben Carsley's Fantasy Take: Whereas there's just enough in Toglia's profile to intrigue me despite the first base profile, Lavigne is too limited to a power-only play for my tastes. He's worth monitoring as he ascends the minors, but I'm not ready to invest yet.

10

Karl Kauffmann   RHP   OFP: 50   ETA: 2021-22
Born: 08/15/97   Age: 22   Bats: R   Throws: R   Height: 6'2"   Weight: 200
Origin: Round 2, 2019 Draft (#77 overall)

The Report: The Rockies Comp Balance B pick, Kauffmann is a bulldog who attacked Big Ten hitters with a power sinker/slider combo. The fastball generally sits in an average velocity band, although he can tick it up into the mid-90s, and it features good sink and run down in the zone. His mid-80s slider features good late tilt and plays well off the fastball, and Kauffmann is comfortable throwing either pitch to either side of the plate. There's not really a changeup at present, and there's a bit of late effort in the delivery that might eventually doom Kauffmann to relief, but he has two present, quality major league offerings and should move quickly in whatever role that Rockies tab for him.

Variance: Medium. Kauffmann pitched deep into the summer during Michigan's College World Series run, so he has no pro track record to speak of yet. There's the usual pitcher risks here, but it's a very polished two-pitch repertoire already.

Ben Carsley's Fantasy Take: First of all, terrible name. Second of all, this is a hard no for dynasty leaguers. A hard no.

The Next Ten

11

Brenton Doyle   OF
Born: 05/14/98   Age: 22   Bats: R   Throws: R   Height: 6'3"   Weight: 200
Origin: Round 4, 2019 Draft (#129 overall)

A fourth rounder out of Division II Shepherd University, Doyle absolutely dominated the Mountain East Conference his junior year. It's a bit of an unusual swing, as the tall, lanky outfielder is almost stooped over at the plate in an open stance. It's unorthodox, but Doyle is athletic enough to make it work. He struggled some with pro spin, but overall offers a solid power/speed combo that reminds me a little bit of Brandon Marsh. Doyle's on the raw side compared to Marsh—and he's only six months younger—so there may be a bit of longer lead time here than your typical college outfield pick, but the rewards might be an every day outfielder, and we might find more in the tank once he gets additional pro reps under his belt.

12

Julio Carreras   IF
Born: 01/12/00   Age: 20   Bats: R   Throws: R   Height: 6'2"   Weight: 190
Origin: International Free Agent, 2018

It's a bit of a double standard that I am intrigued by Carreras's profile. You could levy many of the same charges here that I did for Colton Welker above. The swing features a big leg kick and a violent uppercut, coupled with plus bat speed. Carreras is rawer at the plate than Welker—not that it should be surprising given their relative experience levels—and struggles with spin both in and out of the zone. It may look a lot like Colton Welker in a few years if he makes it to Double-A. He may not make it to Double-A. I think Carreras does though.

I'm more willing to bet on this swing when it's attached to this kind of athletic, projectable frame. Carreras is quick-twitch and an above-average runner. Despite the rawness at the plate, he's a smooth infielder with the arm for the left side. The variance is extreme here given his lack of pro reps or amateur pedigree, but he's already started to get results on the field and the tools aren't too shabby either.

13 Jacob Wallace RHP
Born: 08/13/98 Age: 21 Bats: R Throws: R Height: 6'1" Weight: 190
Origin: Round 3, 2019 Draft (#100 overall)

Wallace puts every bit of his 6-foot-1, 190-pound frame into every pitch. He can ramp it up mid-90s and higher with the fastball, but the uptempo delivery, and long, bordering on violent arm action, means his fastball command will struggle to bump average. He offers a power slider that flashes good depth as well, so yeah, we are already in the 95-and-a-slider part of this list. Wallace should move fast as a pen arm, and could help the MLB bullpen as soon as this year, although as a UConn pitcher, he was used very heavily late into last spring, so it's worth monitoring his stuff and health going forward. Assuming he stays healthy though, he could be an eighth inning arm in short order.

14 Riley Pint RHP [this space left intentionally blank]
Born: 11/06/97 Age: 22 Bats: R Throws: R Height: 6'5" Weight: 225
Origin: Round 1, 2016 Draft (#4 overall)

Man, f*** if I know. We've slotted Pint in with a group of relief prospects without closer upside, which represents a precipitous fall for the former fourth-overall pick. He came back from a 2018 forearm injury and promptly walked 31 batters in 23 innings before being shut down in June with shoulder tendonitis. The control issues aren't hard to spot. Pint's delivery is max effort and he struggles badly to find a consistent release point. If he ever does figure it out, he has far more late-inning upside than those around him with triple-digit heat and a plus breaker in his holster. But for a second straight year we must confess, he probably isn't exactly the 14th-best prospect in the system, or if he is, one standard deviation could put him fourth or 44th. In a better system I'd write him off the list until there's some glimmer that it might maybe, possibly, sort of be coming together, but even a longshot upside bet is worth it in Colorado.

15   Ashton Goudeau   RHP
Born: 07/23/92   Age: 27   Bats: R   Throws: R   Height: 6'6"   Weight: 205
Origin: Round 27, 2012 Draft (#823 overall)

Now, putting a 27-year-old, recent minor league free agent on your prospect list generally signals to the reader that this is not a very good system. And yes, this is not a very good system, but Goudeau is a prospect, and age ain't nothing but a number. I tend to be less concerned about age-relative-to-league with pitchers, but yeah, a 27-year-old who spent most of the season as a Double-A starter is not usually going to keep my notebook open for that long. But Goudeau found something in his third organization, dominating upper minors hitters with a lively plus fastball that comes from a tough angle given his 6-foot-6 height and high-three-quarters slot. There's some deception in the delivery as well. Goudeau pairs it with an 11-6 curve with late bite that's effective at the bottom of the zone when playing off the riding fastball. The below-average change, occasional command problems, and violent at times mechanics probably limit Goudeau to the pen, and the Rockies moved him there shortly after his promotion to Triple-A, but there's setup potential in the stuff at present. That's useful even if he might technically qualify as an older millennial.

16   Ben Bowden   LHP
Born: 10/21/94   Age: 25   Bats: L   Throws: L   Height: 6'4"   Weight: 235
Origin: Round 2, 2016 Draft (#45 overall)

Bowden is in some ways the left-handed version of Wallace, all the way down to both being from Massachusetts. Bowden is the much larger of the two, and gets to his 95 mph heat a bit easier, from a slingy delivery that's tough on lefties. He dominated Double-A hitters with the fastball and a potential plus tumbling changeup, although he struggled to have consistent feel for the pitch. There's a slurvy slider as well. Bowden's stuff is more low-end setup than high-end, with potential LOOGY risk, but he's also close to ready for the Rockies pen, and continued to miss bats despite getting knocked around in the PCL.

17   Tommy Doyle   RHP
Born: 05/01/96   Age: 24   Bats: R   Throws: R   Height: 6'6"   Weight: 235
Origin: Round 2, 2017 Draft (#70 overall)

Doyle was taken in the second round in 2017 as a college closer out of Virginia, but his pace through the minors has been slow-going. The stuff all checks out. He is a massive human who can run it up into the upper-90s and pairs it with a mid-80s slider that has touched 90 and can be a wipeout swing-and-miss offering when it's on. The command is just okay, the slider rolls sometimes, there's only a theoretical change, and plenty of effort in the delivery. There's—you guessed it—late inning potential here, but Doyle is a bit further away than the relief-only arms ahead of him.

Colorado Rockies 2020

18 Ryan Feltner   RHP
Born: 09/02/96   Age: 23   Bats: R   Throws: R   Height: 6'4"   Weight: 190
Origin: Round 4, 2018 Draft (#126 overall)

The Rockies fourth-round pick out of Ohio State in 2018, Feltner struggled in his pro debut for Asheville, but the stuff was better than the performance—which was a recurring theme for him in college as well. He offers easy mid-90s heat as a starter, with a fastball that could play up in relief—where he's likely to end up. There's a potential above-average, low-80s slider with late two-plane action as well. Is it another 95-and-a-slider guy? Yes it sure is. You'd have preferred to see Feltner handle the South Atlantic League better as a major college arm, so there is more risk in this profile than some of the other reliever arms ahead of him, but he generally slots in the same "potential setup guy" band otherwise.

19 Antonio Santos   RHP
Born: 10/06/96   Age: 23   Bats: R   Throws: R   Height: 6'3"   Weight: 180
Origin: International Free Agent, 2015

Santos is an interesting arm strength flyer. He can run his fastball up into the upper 90s—and sit mid-90s in short bursts—but the pitch tends to run a little true, and a violent finish to his delivery suggests the command profile may not be fine enough to start. He does have a little hitch/hesitation which can create timing issues for the hitters, and he's effectively wild with the heater.

Santos has a full four-pitch mix, but both breaking balls are below-average—a slurvy curveball will occasionally flash decent tilt—and the changeup is inconsistent. The change will at least flash some hard fade and dive, but it's firm, and fastball/changeup relievers are a rare bird. There's some swing/spot start potential here and maybe you can get one of the breakers to average to give him a shot at middle relief, but it's a tough major league profile even before you consider his future home park.

20 Eddy Diaz   IF
Born: 02/14/00   Age: 20   Bats: R   Throws: R   Height: 6'0"   Weight: 175
Origin: International Free Agent, 2017

Diaz was signed out of Cuba for $750,000 in 2017 and made his stateside debut this year in the Pioneer League. He has a slim frame and should fill out some, but he's not a projection monster. He's likely to remain a bit undersized and be a slash and burn guy at the plate, although the wrists are strong and keep the bat from getting knocked out of his hands at present. He's been splitting his time between second and short, although the arm is a better fit for the keystone. He's a smooth, rangy fielder, who should hold his plus speed as he ages. The lack of physicality limits the upside here, and there's a risk that better velocity beats him as he moves up the organizational ladder, but there's a potential speedy bench infielder here at maturity.

Personal Cheeseball

PC

Alan Trejo SS
Born: 05/30/96   Age: 24   Bats: R   Throws: R   Height: 6'2"   Weight: 185
Origin: Round 16, 2017 Draft (#476 overall)

It was pretty slim pickings at my full-season home park this year, but Trejo caught my eye early on as at least a player worth keeping tabs on. He's a pretty slick defensive shortstop with some pop, and the Rockies continued to get him reps at second and third. The hit and power tools are both on the wrong side of average, but he's a good athlete and smart baserunner. He can be a bit of a red ass, as he has strong opinions on things like "the strike zone" and "whether or not that was a check swing." It does liven up the proceedings on a cold spring night in Hartford. It's a crowded infield in Coors right now even before you get to the Rox bevvy of infield prospects above Trejo on this list, but the shortstop glove gives him a chance for major league employment at some point.

Low Minors Sleeper

LMS

Mitchell Kilkenny RHP
Born: 03/24/97   Age: 23   Bats: R   Throws: R   Height: 6'4"   Weight: 206
Origin: Round 2C, 2018 Draft (#76 overall)

Kilkenny, the Rockies second-round pick in 2018, had Tommy John surgery shortly after the draft. He was back on a Pioneer League mound in 2019 for what amounted to more or less an extended rehab assignment. The command down in the zone of the sinking fastball and slider were solid for a pitcher only a little over a year removed from going under the knife. 2020 will put him over 20 months out TJ, and we'll have more of an idea of what the stuff will look like going forward with a full-season ball assignment and fewer restrictions on his usage. If the low-90s, touch 95 velocity comes all the way back, Kilkenny profiles as a backend starter or setup man out of the pen.

Top Talents 25 and Under (as of 4/1/2020)

1. German Marquez
2. Brendan Rodgers
3. Ryan McMahon
4. Garrett Hampson
5. Ryan Rolison
6. Ryan Vilade
7. Terrin Vavra
8. Peter Lambert

Colorado Rockies 2020

9. Antonio Senzatela
10. Michael Toglia

Folks, I won't lie to you—it's bleak. How bleak? So bleak I considered bending the rules to allow David Dahl (who, celebrating his 26th birthday on April 1st, is by the barest measure ineligible for this exercise) on the list. So bleak that when the deed was done I briefly panicked with Craig about if the Rockies are the next Orioles. So bleak that after having been reassured things aren't quite there yet, I still initially titled my google doc "Orioles 25U."

How did we get here? Fitting for the Rockies, let's go bottom up:

Lambert and Senzatela are here and in their quests for rotation spots united—as massive underperformers who remain in the running by default, being that there is no one in the wings to supplant them and wake up the Rockies from their Evanescence-backed nightmare.

If you think Hampson is where McMahon stood a year ago, there's good and bad news—after flirting with replacement-level in parts of two seasons, McMahon broke through last season as an average regular. The downside? It doesn't look like McMahon, in his last year of eligibility for this list, has another gear in him. With Hampson lumped into the same age bracket, time is running out for him to prove even that capability.

Finally, Marquez is almost everything a team wants atop its rotation—young, great and showing flashes of more to come, cost-controlled on a deal that now looks ludicrously team-friendly—all Marquez can do to improve in 2020 is stay healthy (and ideally benefit from better batted ball luck).

At least there's one legitimate star in this group. But friends, I just don't see it.

Part 3: Featured Articles

The Baseball Is Juiced (Again)

Robert Arthur

This article originally appeared at Baseball Prospectus on April 5, 2019.

It started when the normally reliable Chris Sale got lit up for three homers by the Mariners in the Red Sox's season opener. It was part of a record number of taters that flew on Opening Day, as starters from Sale to Zack Greinke were taken deep by the handful. Then Christian Yelich hit a home run in each of his first four games, tying yet another MLB record, this one for consecutive games with a dinger to start a season.

It didn't take long for fans and players to begin whispering and tweeting about the baseballs being juiced again. It's early yet for us to come to any definitive conclusion about the 2019 season, but preliminary data shows that the baseball has returned to its aerodynamic peak. Whether that means this season will smash home run records like 2017 did remains to be seen.

Before home run explosion over the last few years, no one worried too much about the baseball's air resistance. While MLB and Rawlings (the company that manufactures the official baseballs) kept track of dozens of metrics to make sure that the ball was consistent from month to month, they didn't measure drag.

But drag is incredibly important in determining how likely a hitter is to knock one out of the park. As baseballs become more aerodynamic, they travel further given a certain initial velocity. A deep fly ball that might have been caught at the warning track can instead go into the first row of the stands. A three percent change in drag coefficient can work to add about five feet to a well-hit fly ball, which can in turn increase home runs league wide by an astounding 10-15 percent.

It's possible to measure the aerodynamics of the baseball using the pitch-tracking radars currently in place in each MLB ballpark. By calculating the loss of speed from when the pitch is released to when it crosses the plate, you can directly measure the drag coefficient on the baseball. I first wrote about the role of decreasing drag in boosting home runs in 2017, and MLB's commission of scientists and statisticians later confirmed that the more aerodynamic baseballs in use that year were largely to blame for the spike in home runs. The same commission rejected some alternate hypotheses, like rising temperatures and a league-wide boost in launch angle pushing more balls over the fence.

The current era has featured some large fluctuations in drag coefficient, leading to first an explosion in 2016 and 2017, and then a dialing back of homers last year. Curious about the record-breaking home run tallies in the last few days, I used the same methodology to measure the aerodynamics of the baseballs so far in 2019.

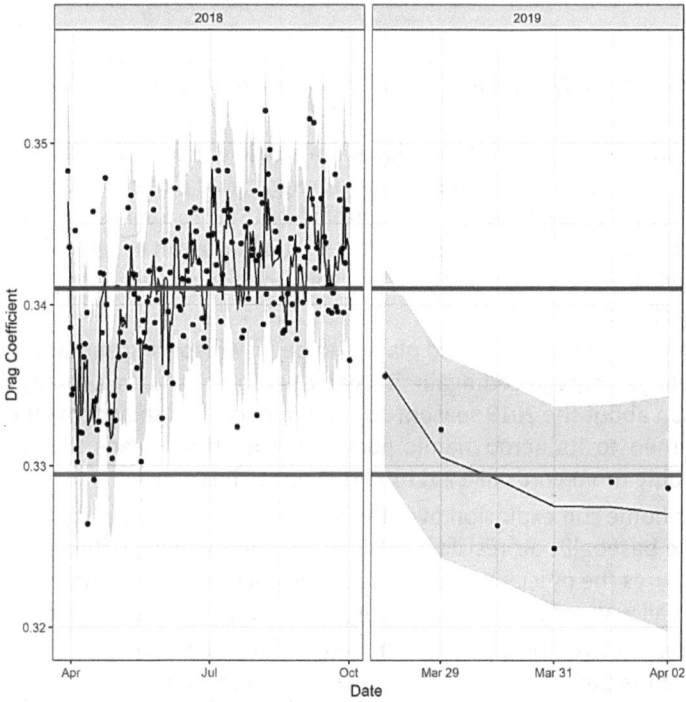

We're only a week into the 2019 season, but the drag numbers so far are among the lowest recorded in the last calendar year. With apologies for gory math, the current 2019 season average drag coefficient (the red line) would be below the 95 percent credible interval (the shaded area) for about nine-tenths of the 2018 season. (I used a Bayesian Random Walk model implemented in INLA to calculate these credible intervals, averaging the drag numbers in each game and adjusting for park.)

There were only a handful of six-day stretches in 2018 that had drag numbers below what we're seeing now, and most were in late June and early July. All of this means that 2019's data so far is quite a bit different than what we saw through most of last year.

These drag coefficients factor out the effects of temperature and air density, so they aren't a product of April cold. However, the numbers could be deceptive if the radars used to track pitches have changed from year to year. I consulted with some experts within baseball who were not aware of any specific modifications to the radar this year that could produce this pattern, but it's an important caveat of which to be aware.

On the one hand, it's only been six days, and we don't quite have the statistical basis to say that these drag coefficients are unprecedented compared to 2018. On the other hand, we've witnessed about 5,000 fastballs so far this season, so it's not as if our sample size is small. At least so far, the baseball has played like it's much more aerodynamic than it was last year. In fact, the current drag coefficient is really only comparable to 2017, when the baseballs were more aerodynamic than they had been in at least a decade.

It's not just fancy radar tracking indicating that the baseball is flying through the air more easily. The current number of home runs per game (as of this writing) is the highest it's been since the heady days of 2017, the year that teams and players broke dinger-related records everywhere you looked. That's especially remarkable considering that we're in what is typically the coldest part of the regular season, when lower temperatures and higher winds tend to suppress offense and keep balls in the air within the park. Comparing only from April to April, this year's rate of home runs per fly ball is even a little bit higher than it was in 2017.

With that said, the current measurements are no guarantee that 2019 will be another year of record-shattering homer hitting. The trouble with the drag measurements is that they are not consistent from June to August, from week to week, or even sometimes from day to day. Whether because of natural manufacturing variation or differences in the underlying supplies of cowhide and thread that go into the baseballs, drag has a tendency to fluctuate up and down over the course of a year. So the homers that fly in the first week of April wouldn't necessarily clear the fence a week later.

It's possible that this one-week drop in drag coefficient subsides and the baseball returns to its 2018 levels. On the other hand, it's almost equally probable that the ball becomes even more slippery and flies ever farther. Either way, it's clear that the baseball's air resistance is something to keep an eye on for the remainder of the 2019 season.

—*Robert Arthur is an author of Baseball Prospectus.*

The Moral Hazard of Playing It Safe

Craig Goldstein

This article originally appeared at Baseball Prospectus on August 6, 2019.

A couple days prior to the trade deadline, amidst a sea of tranquility posing as the lead up to the trade deadline, Bob Nightengale took to Twitter. Nightengale, who was probably wearing his pants backwards at the time, tweeted that MLB GMs were coming around on the idea that the unified trade deadline should be moved back from July 31 to August 15, so they could better assess their positions in the standings and whether they should buy or sell. To which I said:

This might strike some as reductive and churlish. And it might be that, but it isn't really wrong, either. Jeff Quinton wrote a great piece discussing the environmental factors that enable front offices to avoid risk without upsetting the apple cart within their own fanbases. I don't believe that it goes far enough, however. His article gives us the proper framework through which to understand why these behaviors have been allowed to seep into front offices throughout the league. Understanding the reasons behind these actions are different from excusing them, though, and GMs should not be let off the hook for their non-competitive approach to the trade deadline (much less the offseason).

⚾   ⚾   ⚾

It's fair to say that fans as a group have rarely, if ever, been pro-player. It is also fair to say that in the time during and following the Moneyball revolution, the pendulum swung from fans who cared intensely about winning in the moment (and thus might be intolerant of a rebuilding approach) to fans who supported building a team that could compete throughout multiple seasons, viewing the playoffs as a crapshoot, with the thought that getting multiple bites at the apple was a better approach than taking a bigger bite in any one season.

There's nothing wrong with that approach, and I still find merit in that argument. However, it seems that the pendulum has swung too far in that direction. Teams are overvaluing some of the individual factors that make themselves long-term contenders rather than attempting to seize a championship when given the opportunity. It's a difficult needle to thread.

And surely, they (and those in similar positions) would have liked another two weeks to clarify where they stand so as to better marshal their resources. We've all asked for a few more minutes when staring at a menu. But all of these GMs and front office personnel are where they are to make difficult decisions. They have proprietary data and internal analysts dedicated to understanding their position relative to the rest of the league, and how any move in the here and now impacts their long-term vision. To complain (if that report is accurate) that over half the season is not enough to properly assess their season is bullshit of the highest order. Move the deadline, and you'd simply have increasingly discounted trade offers because teams would be acquiring even less control of anyone they're acquiring, rental or not.

Major league front offices are behaving like the managers they lampooned two decades ago. They're effectively sacrificing a runner to second in the ninth inning—not because it's the correct move, but rather because it is safe. It used to be that the phrase "moral hazard" was used to describe general managers who made ill-fated, short-sighted decisions aimed at locking in wins and securing their jobs at the expense of their team's future. Now, general managers are guilty of committing moral hazards in the opposite direction, playing it utterly safe and terrified of becoming scapegoats.

In lieu of bold action, they opt to pussyfoot around a current window of contention, choosing instead to play the long game and stack up years of control like they're blocks in a game of Jenga. GMs pass on signing quality players in free agency because the back-end of the deal might look bad, and because they might be able to squeeze out 70 percent of the production from a player who costs a tenth as much. That's a safer investment, too, because it's also hard to prove a negative—it's impossible to prove that Manny Machado would make the Mets a playoff team in 2019-2020, but it's easy to say that the back half of Robinson Cano's contract sucks. Owners, who rule over GM's jobs, are also humans with human brain processes that will always make the so-called albatross contract uglier than the road not taken.

These days, GMs are remembered for the bad deals they make and the surplus value they generate, not the acquisition of expensive, necessary talents that meet their market worth (or fall slightly short while still providing significant on-field value). And front offices know that one or two expensive misfires can cost them their jobs, no matter how many good deals they make.

No front office exemplifies this ethos more than the Toronto Blue Jays. General Manager Ross Atkins had this to say following the Blue Jays underwhelming trade deadline:

This is by no means the first time that an executive will cite years of control to justify their actions, which is often just another way of saying "don't look at what we got, look at how much we got of it." Atkins touts quantity to elide the discussion of quality—either, that of the players acquired, or those given up. Remember: the other teams presumably value years of control, too.

Atkins also had some thoughts to offer regarding free agents back in early 2018:

This ignores, of course, whether the player can create enough value in the front end of a contract to justify the longer term of a deal, and the decline that often occurs in the back end. It also ignores whether the player can fill a need the team requires and put them in a position to compete for and win a championship. But as teams seemingly avoid contention at all, where they might end up having to consider and later justify some of these tough decisions, we still see risk-averse approaches.

Anthony Fenech's article on two trades that recently extended GM Al Avila didn't make got at this issue rather well:

> Passing on those deals was defensible: Both players had yet to break out and trading [Michael] Fulmer—a pitcher who appeared to be a future ace, no matter his injury concerns—would have taken serious gumption, opening Avila up to strong criticism.

Avoiding strong criticism is something each of us can understand as a motivation, but the avoidance of criticism only matters if that criticism is valid. In Fulmer's case, shoving his injury concerns aside affects not only the years that the team controls him (he is currently missing a full season due to Tommy John surgery) but also the quality of those seasons, as his knee and elbow injuries combined to dampen his effectiveness even when healthy enough to pitch. But it was easy to present the then-current image of Fulmer as a top of the rotation pitcher who the team had under its domain for the next five seasons as something to build around. The status quo isn't nearly as often second-guessed as a decision that disrupts it.

⚾ ⚾ ⚾

MLB GMs are risk-averse to a fault. They are ivy-educated and consulting firm-approved, and yet they can't seem to avoid leaving wins on the table in their all-consuming lust for a non-existent $/WAR championship. They are supposed to zig when everyone else zags, and not merely pay lip service to the idea of zigging through a calculated PR plan built on convincing the fan base their approach is novel when it actually apes most of their competitors. Instead they've become far more concerned with making safe, accepted-by-the-new-common-wisdom decisions, such that our prior understanding of what a moral hazard is has become inverted.

I can't blame them entirely, and not only because of the reasons that Quinton illuminated in his article, but also because of the damage wrought by the introduction of the second wild card (WC2) spot. MLB's desire to have more teams in playoff contention has sparked anti-competitive behavior. Teams know now that they do not need to swing big as they assemble their roster because there is a good chance that a mediocre team can either catch fire and capture a division, or muddle along until they back into the WC2.

Simultaneously, the one-game playoff has neutered the WC1, putting an entire season on the flip of a coin like some sort of baseball-obsessed Anton Chigurh. While the one-game playoff makes sense as a way to increase the value of winning a division, it also means that if a front office doesn't like its chances of overcoming a behemoth like the Dodgers or Astros in the offseason, they have few incentives to chase glory. Similarly, the relative inaction in the NL Central at the trade deadline—despite a wide open division—can be explained by the idea that any high-variance investment could still result in only a wild card (or worse) result, given the mere two months left in the season to make an impact.

⚾   ⚾   ⚾

As stated at the top, we should not confuse reasons for excuses. The implementation of the second wild card is just one of many environmental factors that influence how each front office operates. I am convinced that it is one of the larger factors, but I am also convinced that organizations need to shed the yoke of "efficiency at all costs" so that they can instead pursue competition, as the spirit of the game intends. Until they do, we're all deadline losers.

—*Craig Goldstein is an author of Baseball Prospectus.*

Index of Names

Almonte, Yency 54
Alonso, Yonder 20
Arenado, Nolan 22
Blackmon, Charlie 24
Bowden, Ben 92, 109
Butera, Drew 26
Carreras, Julio 95, 107
Castellani, Ryan 97
Dahl, David 28
Davis, Wade 56
Daza, Yonathan 95
Desmond, Ian 30
Diaz, Eddy 95, 110
Díaz, Elias 32
Díaz, Jairo 60
Diehl, Phillip 58
Doyle, Brenton 95, 107
Doyle, Tommy 109
Dunn, Mike 97
Estévez, Carlos 62
Feltner, Ryan 110
Freeland, Kyle 64
Fuentes, Josh 95
Garcia, Rico 97
González, Chi Chi 66
Goudeau, Ashton 97, 109
Gray, Jon 68
Guillen, Alexander 97
Hampson, Garrett 34
Harvey, Joe 97
Hilliard, Sam 36, 104

Hoffman, Jeff 70
Iannetta, Chris 95
Johnson, DJ 72
Kauffmann, Karl 107
Kilkenny, Mitchell 97, 111
Kinley, Tyler 97
Lambert, Peter 74
Lavigne, Grant 95, 106
Lawrence, Justin 97
Márquez, German 80
McGee, Jake 76
McMahon, Ryan 38
Melville, Tim 78
Murphy, Daniel 40
Musgrave, Harrison 97
Nevin, Tyler 89
Nuñez, Dom 90
Oberg, Scott 83
Oh, Seunghwan 97
Owings, Chris 42
Parsons, Wes 97
Pazos, James 97
Pint, Riley 93, 108
Ramos, Roberto 95
Reynolds, Mark 95
Rodgers, Brendan 44, 101
Rolison, Ryan 94, 102
Rusin, Chris 97
Santos, Antonio 97, 110
Schunk, Aaron 95, 105
Senzatela, Antonio 85

Shaw, Bryan	87	Trejo, Alan	111
Stamets, Eric	95	Vavra, Terrin	95, 103
Story, Trevor	46	Vilade, Ryan	91, 102
Tapia, Raimel	48	Wallace, Jacob	108
Tinoco, Jesus	97	Welker, Colton	50, 105
Toglia, Michael	95, 104	Wolters, Tony	52